GRAYWOLF PRESS

1993

THE OWL
IN THE MASK
OF THE DREAMER
COLLECTED POEMS
BY JOHN HAINES

[signature: John Haines]

POEMS FROM:

Winter News
The Stone Harp
Twenty Poems
Leaves and Ashes
In Five Years' Time
Cicada
In a Dusty Light
News from the Glacier
New Poems, 1980–88
New and Uncollected Poems

GRAYWOLF PRESS

Many of the poems in this volume were previously published in *Winter News* (Wesleyan University Press, 1966, revised in 1983); *The Stone Harp* (Wesleyan University Press, 1971); *Twenty Poems* (Unicorn Press, 1971); *Leaves and Ashes* (Kayak Press, 1974); *In Five Years' Time* (Smokeroot Press, 1976); *Cicada* (Wesleyan University Press, 1977); *News from the Glacier: Selected Poems 1960–1980* (Wesleyan University Press, 1982); *New Poems: 1980–88* (Story Line Press, 1990). The author gratefully acknowledges the editors of the following periodicals, in which many of the poems in Part VIII of this book first appeared: *Alea, The Amicus Journal, The Atlantic, Green Mountains Review, The Hudson Review, Michigan Quarterly Review, New England Review,* and *The New Virigina Review.*

Publication of this volume is made possible in part by a grant provided by the Minnesota State Arts Board through an appropriation by the Minnesota State Legislature, and by a grant from the National Endowment for the Arts. Additional support has been provided by the Jerome Foundation, the Mellon Foundation, the Lila Wallace-Reader's Digest Fund, the McKnight Foundation, the Dayton-Hudson Foundation for Dayton's and Target stores, the Cowles Media Foundation, the General Mills Foundation, and other generous contributions from foundations, corporations, and individuals. Graywolf Press is a member agency of United Arts, Saint Paul. To these organizations and individuals who make our work possible, we offer heartfelt thanks.

Published by GRAYWOLF PRESS
2402 University Avenue, Saint Paul, Minnesota 55114.
All rights reserved. Printed in the United States of America.

9   8   7   6   5   4   3   2
First Printing, 1993
Second Printing, 1994

Library of Congress Cataloging-in-Publication Data

Haines, John Meade, 1924—
    The owl in the mask of the dreamer : collected poems / John Haines
        p.   cm.
    "Poems from: Winter news, The stone harp, Twenty poems, Leaves and ashes, In five years' time, Cicada, News from the glacier, new and uncollected poems, New poems, 1980–88."
    ISBN 1-55597-184-9 (cloth : acid-free paper)
    I. Title
PS3558.A33A6   1993
811'.54—dc20   93-14645

TO THE MEMORY OF

GUSTAVO MOTTA

(1944–1993)

CONTENTS

I. *from* WINTER NEWS (1966)

II. *from* THE STONE HARP (1971)

III. *from* TWENTY POEMS (1971)

IV. INTERIM: *Uncollected Poems from the 1970s*

V. *from* C I C A D A (1977)

VI. *from* NEWS FROM THE GLACIER (1982)

VII. *from* NEW POEMS 1980–88 (1990)

VIII. NEW AND UNCOLLECTED POEMS (1993)

THE OWL
IN THE MASK
OF THE DREAMER

PREFACE

The poems collected in this volume represent the better part of the work I have done in verse from 1958 until the present. Inevitably, I have had to make difficult decisions, and not all the poems I think worth saving are included. There are, on the other hand, one or two poems I might have discarded long ago but for the fact that now and then someone will tell me how much that particular poem has meant to them. I have, accordingly, made the best choice available to me under the conditions of space, format, and continuity.

With few exceptions, the poems are presented as they were first written and in their original published sequence. The exceptions are those poems that were at the time of first publication not entirely satisfying to me and have since been substantially revised. An example of this is the poem entitled "To The Wall," first published in the early 1970s, and then within the past year or two revised so that I have been able to see it as a new poem. A more extreme example, "The Poem Without Meaning," first appeared as a much shorter poem in an issue of the *Hudson Review* in 1966. Since that time I have completely rewritten the poem. But such instances are few.

The sections into which the book is divided reflect, each in its own way, the time, place, and circumstances in which the poems were written. *Winter News* was born of the isolation in which I then lived – that remote, largely self-contained world of the forest, of snow and animal life, of hunting and gathering – and into which news of the outside world penetrated even so. What I wrote then emerged with difficulty from a kind of spell, one that I was reluctant to break, knowing that once I did, nothing would ever be quite the same. By the time I came to write the poems of *The Stone Harp,* many things had changed, and the spell had been broken. The outside world of public events, of politics and history and, to an extent, of professional necessity, intruded more and more. I re-entered, reluctantly yet necessarily, the world I had left behind many years before. This re-encounter was for me drastic and unsettling, and for some time I found it difficult to write new poems, and certainly never again in the mode of *Winter News*.

The Stone Harp seems to me now to be a rather harsh and difficult book, but considering the time in which most of the poems were written, perhaps the bleakness of tone will be understandable. The poems reflect, at times obliquely, many of the national and international events we have lived through in recent decades: the Cuban Missile Crisis, the Vietnam War – the entire period of 1960s, with its social unrest, its anti-war demonstrations, and the death of a figure like Che Guevara which affected me profoundly. Here as elsewhere, the poems also reflect the reading I was absorbed in at the time of writing. An early poem in *Winter News,* "The End of the Summer," could not have been written as it stands had I not been reading Boris Pasternak's *Doctor Zhivago*, with its images of flight and disorder, of armed partisans camped in the Siberian forest. Similarly, the concluding poem in *The Stone Harp*, "The Flight," reflects directly my reading of Mikhail Sholokov's novels of the turbulent Civil War period in Russia, with their images of deserted villages, of a people uprooted and driven on the roads.

That part of this book subtitled INTERIM represents a period when I was on the move, teaching at one school or another, in search of a settled situation, and unable to complete many of the poems I was working on. Not until 1977, while living in England, did I feel ready to publish another substantial collection, *Cicada*. During that period also most of the poems included in *News from the Glacier* were completed and collected under the title *In a Dusty Light*.

I have not always made the customary distinction between my poems in verse and my writing in prose. There are pages in my memoir, *The Stars, the Snow, the Fire,* that seem to me, except for their sentence structure, to be poetry and of a continuity with my poems in verse. In this regard, I have often thought of the German word for poet, *Dichter,* which does not automatically distinguish, as does our English word, *poet,* between the writer of verse and the writer of prose. Rather, it appears to be a more inclusive term, one that stands for the serious creative writer generally, essayist as well as novelist. It is a fact, though I will not attempt to prove it here, that many of the epic poems of our time have been conceived and written, not in verse but in the form of the novel. I am thinking of writers like Hermann Broch and Robert Musil, of Thomas Mann and Jean Giono, among others, in whose major prose works a poetic intensity and an epic quality are sometimes achieved and sustained.

Collecting these poems has not been easy, for I have had to relive many of their occasions and events – the times, places, and persons invoked – much of which is now lost. In other words, it has not been merely a matter of making a list, of discarding and selecting, but of something deeper and more complicated. I have at one time or another written about a few of these poems, brief essays giving an account of how the poem came to be written, its background, and so forth. I suppose an entire book might be made of such things, and it would not necessarily be frivolous or self-indulgent to do so. I am aware also, in reading through this collection, of a prevailing somberness, of a tone that might be called elegiac. All I can say is that the author has seen life and experience in a certain way, has seen human history as it appears to him, and not otherwise.

I have to thank here many people, not all of whom can be named, for the list would be too long. They are people whose presence in my life, for one reason or another, made it possible, even necessary, for the poems to be written. Among them, Jo Haines, who shared so many years of work and quiet at Richardson. Leslie Sennett, for her companionship in England and Montana. My step-children, Blair, Anne, Karen, and Peter, for what they gave me at a critical time. Jo Going, for her insights and sustained confidence in these poems. Additionally, my publishers at Graywolf Press, and at Story Line Press; Wesleyan University Press for having kept so many of my books in print over the years; editors and friends at the *Hudson Review* and *Ohio Review,* among the many publications where these poems first found acceptance. My colleagues and students at Ohio University, at George Washington University, at the University of Cincinnati, and elsewhere for their welcome and support.

And, not least, the places where I have lived and within whose boundaries my thoughts have found expression. In the end, I suppose, it is just those places, with all that they embody and represent, with their configurations, their histories and their people, that have made the difference. Had I not chosen years ago to return to Alaska and the life I had tentatively begun there, I would have become a very different man and writer.

Commonplace ambition aside, the motivation that turns one's life toward poetry and sustains it, remains, as it must, a mystery. The commitment once made, everything that enters our life, that touches us, sometimes briefly, at times profoundly, changes us and adds to that power, latent and intermittent though it may be, by which, as Wordsworth put it, "we see into the life of things." With all of its difficulties and successes, the losses and displacements that are implied, I can think of no better justification for having lived and written as I have.

JOHN HAINES
January 1993

Yet there remains with us the feeling
that all poetry and all intellectual
life were once the handmaids of
the holy, and have passed through
the temple.

— JACOB BURCKHARDT

Part I

WINTER NEWS

1966

IF THE OWL CALLS AGAIN

at dusk
from the island in the river,
and it's not too cold,

I'll wait for the moon
to rise,
then take wing and glide
to meet him.

We will not speak,
but hooded against the frost
soar above
the alder flats, searching
with tawny eyes.

And then we'll sit
in the shadowy spruce
and pick the bones
of careless mice,

while the long moon drifts
toward Asia
and the river mutters
in its icy bed.

And when the morning climbs
the limbs
we'll part without a sound,

fulfilled, floating
homeward as
the cold world awakens.

(1960)

WINTER NEWS

They say the wells
are freezing
at Northway where
the cold begins.

Oil tins bang
as evening comes on,
and clouds of
steaming breath drift
in the street.

Men go out to feed
the stiffening dogs,

the voice of the snowman
calls the white-
haired children home.

POEM OF THE FORGOTTEN

I came to this place,
a young man green and lonely.

Well quit of the world,
I framed a house of moss and timber,
called it a home,
and sat in the warm evenings
singing to myself as a man sings
when he knows there is no one to hear.

I made my bed under the shadow
of leaves, and awoke
in the first snow of autumn,
filled with silence.

THE MOLE

Sometimes I envy those
who spring like great black-
and-gold butterflies
before the crowded feet
of summer –
              brief, intense,
like pieces of the sun,
they are remembered and celebrated
long after night has fallen.

But I believe also in one
who in the dead of winter
tunnels through a damp,
clinging darkness,
nosing the soil of old gardens.

He lives unnoticed, but
deep within him there is a dream
of the surface one day
breaking and crumbling:

and a small, brown-furred
figure stands there,
blinking at the sky,
as the rising sun slowly dries
his strange, unruly wings.

FAIRBANKS UNDER THE SOLSTICE

Slowly, without sun, the day sinks
toward the close of December.
It is minus sixty degrees.

Over the sleeping houses a dense
fog rises – smoke from banked fires,
and the snowy breath of an abyss

through which the cold town
is perceptibly falling.

As if Death were a voice made visible,
with the power of illumination . . .

Now, in the white shadow
of those streets, ghostly newsboys
make their rounds, delivering
to the homes of those
who have died of the frost
word of the resurrection of Silence.

(1962)

THE HOUSE OF THE INJURED

I found a house in the forest,
small, windowless, and dark.

From the doorway came the close,
suffocating odor of blood
and fur mixed with dung.

I looked inside and saw
an injured bird
that filled the room.

With a stifled croaking
it lunged toward the door
as if held back
by an invisible chain:

the beak was half eaten away,
and its heart beat wildly
under the rumpled feathers.

I sank to my knees –
a man shown the face of God.

FOREBODING

Something immense and lonely
divides the earth at evening.

For nine years I have watched
from an inner doorway:
as in a confused vision,
manlike figures approach, cover
their faces, and pass on,
heavy with iron and distance.

There is no sound but the wind
crossing the road, filling
the ruts with a dust as fine as chalk.

Like the closing of an inner door,
the day begins its dark
journey, across nine bridges
wrecked one by one.

TO TURN BACK

The grass people bow
their heads before the wind.

How would it be
to stand among them, bending
our heads like that ... ?

Yes ... and no ... perhaps ...
lifting our dusty faces
as if we were waiting for
the rain ... ?

The grass people stand
all year, patient and obedient –

to be among them
is to have only simple
and friendly thoughts,

and not be afraid.

THE INVASION

In the far north the sea
is beginning to freeze,
and groups of men are
gathering on the stony shore
in a white dust of snow.

Their bodies are heavy with furs.
They have strong brown faces,
and eyes used to
looking into great distances.

From small fires built among them,
thin smoke mingles
with the guttural language
they speak and blows
away toward the south...

AND WHEN THE GREEN MAN COMES

The man is clothed
in birchbark,
small birds cling to his limbs
and one builds
a nest in his ear.

The clamor of bedlam
infests his hair, a wind
blowing in his head

shakes down
a thought that turns
to moss and lichen
at his feet.

His eyes are blind
with April,
his breath distilled
of butterflies
and bees, and in his beard
the maggot sings.

He comes again
with litter of chips
and empty cans,
his shoes full of mud and dung;

an army of shedding dogs
attends him,
the valley shudders where
he stands,
   redolent of roses,
exalted in
the streaming rain.

A MOOSE CALLING

Who are you,
calling me in the dusk,

O dark shape
with heavy horns?

I am neither cow
nor bull –

I walk upright
and carry your death
in my hands.

It is my voice
answers you,

beckoning, deceitful,
ruse of the hunter —

at twilight,
in the yellow frost

I wait for you.

HORNS

I went to the edge of the wood
in the color of evening,
and rubbed with a piece of horn
against a tree,
believing the great, dark moose
would come, his eyes
on fire with the moon.

I fell asleep in an old white tent.
The October moon rose,
and down a wide, frozen stream
the moose came roaring,
hoarse with rage and desire.

I awoke and stood in the cold
as he slowly circled the camp.
His horns exploded in the brush
with dry trees cracking
and falling; his nostrils flared
as, swollen-necked, smelling
of challenge, he stalked by me.

I called him back, and he came
and stood in the shadow
not far away, and gently rubbed
his horns against the icy willows.
I heard him breathing softly.
Then with a faint sigh of warning
soundlessly he walked away.

I stood there in the moonlight,
and the darkness and silence
surged back, flowing around me,
full of a wild enchantment,
as though a god had spoken.

THE MOOSEHEAD

Stripped of its horns and skin,
the moosehead is sinking.

The eyes have fallen back
from their ports into the sleepy,
green marrow of Death.

Over the bridge of the nostrils,
the small pilots of the soil
climb and descend.

In the cabin of the skull,
where the brain once floated
like a ruddy captain,
there is just this black water
and a faint glowing of phosphorus.

VICTIMS

The knife that makes long scars
in the flesh lays bare the bones –

pale trees in the forest of blood
where the birds of life and death
endlessly weave their
nests with straws of anguish.

There, the hunter and his quarry . . .

Parting the branches, the doomed
animal chokes on his own
breath, and sees, as in a red mist,
his own dripping carcass.

DENALI ROAD

By the Denali road, facing
north, a battered chair
in which nothing but the wind
was sitting.
    And farther on
toward evening, an old man
with a vague smile,
his rifle rusting in his arms.

         (1 9 6 2)

THE FIELD OF THE CARIBOU

Moving in a restless exhaustion,
humps of earth that rise
covered with dead hair.

There is no sound from the wind
blowing the tattered velvet
of their antlers.

The grey shepherds of the tundra
pass like islands of smoke,
and I hear only a heavy thumping
as though far in the west
some tired bodies
were falling from a cliff.

ON THE DIVIDE

I am haunted by
the deaths of animals.

Their frozen, moonlit eyes
stare into the hollow
of my skull; they listen
as though I had
something to tell them.

But a shadow rises
at the edge of my dream —

No one speaks;

and afterwhile the cold,
red mantle of dawn
sweeps over our bodies.

BOOK OF THE JUNGLE

The animal, rising at dusk
from its bed in the trampled
grass —
            this is how it all began.

Far off the shaggy tribesmen
listened and fed their fires
with thorns.

Secret paths of the forest,
when did your children walk
unarmed, clothed only
with the shadows of leaves?

We are still kneeling
and listening,
as from the edge of a field
there rises sometimes at evening
the snort of a rutting bull.

DIVIDED, THE MAN IS DREAMING

One half
lives in sunlight; he is
the hunter and calls
the beasts of the field
about him.
Bathed in sweat and tumult
he slakes and kills,
eats meat
and knows blood.

His other half
lies in shadow
and longs for stillness,
a corner of the evening

where birds
rest from flight:
cool grass grows at his feet,
dark mice feed
from his hands.

DESERTED CABIN

Here in the yellowing
aspen grove
on Campbell's Hill
the wind is searching
a fallow garden.

I remember the old man
who lived here.
Five years have gone by,
and his house has grown
to resemble his life –
a shallow cave hung
with old hides, rusty
traps and chains,
smelling of eighty years
of unwashed bedding
and rotting harness.

I see him sitting there
now as he used to,
his starved animals gathered
about his bony knees.
He talks to himself
of poverty, cursing softly,
jabbing a stick
at the shadows.

The bitterness of a soul
that wanted only to walk

in the sun and pick
the ripening berries.

It is like coming home
late in the evening
with a candle in your hand,
and meeting someone
you had forgotten –
the voice is strange.

It is the cold autumn wind
stirring the frozen grass,
as if some life
had just passed there,
bound home
in the early darkness.

PRAYER TO THE SNOWY OWL

Descend, silent spirit;

you whose golden eyes
pierce the grey
shroud of the world –

Marvelous ghost!

Drifter of the arctic night,
destroyer of those
who gnaw in the dark –

preserver of whiteness.

DREAM OF THE LYNX

Beside a narrow trail in the blue
cold of evening the trap is sprung,
and a growling deep in the throat
tells of life risen
to the surface of darkness.

The moon in my dream takes the shape
of animals who walk by its light
and never sleep, whose yellow eyes
are certain of what they seek.

Sinking, floating beneath the eyelid,
the hairy shape of the slayer appears,
a shadow that crouches
hidden in a thicket of alders,
nostrils quivering;
and the ever-deepening track
of the unseen, feeding host.

THE DREAM OF FEBRUARY

I

In the moonlight,
in the heavy snow,
I was hunting along
the sunken road
and heard behind me
the quiet step
and smothered whimper
of something following . . .

Ah, tree of panic
I climbed
to escape the night,
as the furry body glided

beneath, lynx with
steady gaze, and began
the slow ascent.

I I

And dark blue foxes
climbed beside me with
famished eyes that
glowed in the shadows;

I stabbed with
a sharpened stick until
one lay across
the path with entrails
spilled, and
the others melted away.

The dead fox
moved again, his jaws
released the
sound of speech.

I I I

Slowly I toiled
up the rotting stairs
to the cemetery
where my mother lay buried,

to find the open grave
with the coffin
tilted beside it,
and something spilled
from the bottom —

a whiteness that flowed
on the ground
and froze into mist that
enveloped the world.

THE VISITOR

The door is open
and the shaggy frost-fog
bounds across the floor
and wraps itself about my feet.
Restless, it climbs
upon my knees; I feel
its breath deep in my bones.

A spirit in it wants
to draw me out past
the whitening hinges
into the cold, enormous rooms
where it lives.

Out there a flickering pathway
leads to a snowy grave
where something in me
has always wanted to lie.

Then let it take me,
a lost, shivering animal –
eyelids shut fast,
hands folded,
wrapped in a stillness made of
ice and starlit tears.

THE SOUND OF ANIMALS IN THE NIGHT

Dark wings that brush the foliage
above us; the crunch of hoofs
in frost, a river flowing
in the lonely voice of the coyote.

As they walk through the moonlight,

we come and go by the flare
of campfires, full of ghosts
with huge, wounded hearts.

THE TRAVELER

I

Among the quiet people of the frost,
I remember an Eskimo
walking one evening
on the road to Fairbanks.

I I

A lamp full of shadows burned
on the table before us;
the light came as though from far off
through the yellow skin of a tent.

I I I

Thousands of years passed.
People were camped on the bank
of a river, drying fish
in the sun. Women bent over
stretched hides, scraping
in a kind of furry patience.

There were long hunts through
the wet autumn grass,
meat piled high in caches —
a red memory against whiteness.

I V

We were away for a long time.
The footsteps of a man walking alone
on the frozen road from Asia
crunched in the darkness
and were gone.

SNOWY NIGHT

This is like a place
we used to know,
but stranger
and filled with the cold
imagination of a frozen
sea, in which
the moon is anchored
like a ghost
in heavy chains.

STAMPEDE

There are cold, bearded men
laboring through the winter night.
They climb the drifts
of a windy, starlit pass
with iron sleighs, and rough dogs
whining in harness.

Behind them, ships shrouded
in smoke and steam
unload by the light of bonfires.
Mingled with heavy thuds
and the creak of straining tackle,
ghostly voices float slowly upward,
whitening in the cold night air.

Beyond the pass, small boats
lie on the shore of a lake,
half-filled with snow, their thin
sails stiff with ice.
The boatmen are fast asleep,
wrapped in furs and frozen sweat,
dreaming of gold
and the white land of promise.

SOUTH WIND

I dreamed of horses in the night,
invaders with strong, sweating
bodies plunging through the cold.

The stars were suddenly hidden,
but dark manes flowed
with sparks, and on the black,
frozen hills the rushing air
soared like a forest on fire.

The thunder of their passage
broke down the walls of my dream.
I awoke in the ruined kingdom
of frost with a warm wind
blowing my hair, and heard about me
and in the distance
the heavy hoofs still pounding
as the wild, invisible army
overran the north.

POEM FOR A COLD JOURNEY

On the road of the self-
contained traveler I stood
like one to whom the great
announcements are made.

In one hand I held
a hard, dry branch with
bitter, purple fruit;
in the other hand a small,
blue-and-yellow bird
whose closed eyes stared inward
upon a growing darkness.

Listening, I could hear
within myself the snow
that was coming, the sound
of a loud, cold trumpet.

THE TREE

Tree of my life,
you have grown slowly
in the shadows of giants.

Through darkness and solitude
you stretch year by year
toward that strange, clear light
in which the sky is hidden.

In the quiet grain of your
thoughts the inner life
of the forest stirs
like a secret still to be named.

POEM

The immense sadness
of approaching winter
hangs in the air
this cloudy September.

Today a muddy road
filled with leaves, tomorrow
the stiffening earth and
a footprint
glazed with ice.

The sun breaking through
still warm, but the road

deep in shadow;
your hand in mine is cold.

Our berries picked,
the mushrooms gathered,
each of us hides
in his heart a small piece
of this summer,
as mice store their roots
in a place
known only to them.

We believe in the life to come,
when the stark tree
stands in silence above
the blackened leaf;
but now at a bend in the road
to stop and listen:
strange song
of a southbound bird
overflows
in the quiet dusk
from the top
                of that tree.

PICKERS

All day we were bent over,
lifting handfuls of wind and dust.

Scraps of some human conversation
blew by; a coffin on wheels
rolled slowly backward across
the field, and the skinned
bodies of the harvest were loaded.

A red cloud boiling up out
of the darkness became the evening.
Sentinels of a shattered army,
we drank bitter coffee, and spoke
of the field, the light, and the cold.

THE END OF THE SUMMER

I

Let the inhuman, drab machines
patrol the road that leads nowhere,
and the men with Bibles
and speeches come to the door,
asking directions –
we will turn them all away
and be alone.

We will not storm what barricades
they erect on the Cuban beaches,
or set forth on the muddy
imperial water –
at least we shall go to hell
with open faces.

I I

The sun keeps its promises,
sentry in the cloth of departure.
The forest is empty,
the people are gone, the smoky
paths are waiting the feet
of furred and silent soldiers.
Death, the surveyor,
plots his kingdom of snow.

I I I

Subversive leaves, you fall
and litter the camps
of our enemies. Unheard-of-wars

sweep down from distant
mountains, filling
the cemeteries of the unborn.

Survivors beat with pale hands
upon the windows;
their eyelids are closed
and their scars sealed
with gauze against the cold.

I stare across the threshold
of my home and feel the sudden
wind that rises
like the breath from a grave.

(1963)

POEM OF THE WINTRY FISHERMAN

At the foot of October
where the current narrows,
the salmon wait,
burning in the shallows —

blood-red, green and orange,
in the ice-blue glacier water.

Listen! you can hear
the long, slow pull of slush
against the banks,
deep rumble of stones.

I stand alone in the smoking
frost, a long hook poised,
and fling the bright fish up
the pebbled, icy bar
to quiver and lie still,
a sinking fire.

Sometimes the cold eggs spill
in the snow, glowing
like the eyes of foxes who wait
at sundown, when I shoulder
my catch and mount
the frozen twilight homeward.

Along the darkening river,
ravens grip their iron twigs,
shadows of
the hungry, shuddering night.

THAW

This wind is like water
pouring through the passes,
bringing a smell of the south
and the drowned, weedy coast,
a place we've never seen.

Reports of gales and wrecked barges.
Three men lost for days
in an open boat;
the search suspended for
the lonely survivor
who crawls exhausted above
the clutch of the tide,
his hands outstretched to the moon
which sails slowly by.

This water floods over us
and surges far to the west,
to be lost in the frozen
plains of the hunters,
who awaken and listen in darkness,
guarding a smoky candle
against the silent
and relentless cold.

WATCHING THE FIRE

Where are the Red Men?
They should be here. They saw the mound
of skulls glowing on the hearth.

For them the stone lamp flickered
and the drafty cave
was walled with visions.

The stories they told us were true,
we should have believed them:

a woman of brute form nurses her child—
wise eyes in a wrinkled skin,
forehead of horn—

he wears a necklace of fangs
and cries softly for flesh and blood.

LISTENING IN OCTOBER

In the quiet house
a lamp is burning
where the book of autumn
lies open on a table.

There is tea with milk
in heavy mugs,
brown raisin cake, and thoughts
that stir the heart
with the promises of death.

We sit without words,
gazing past the limit
of fire into the towering
darkness. . . .

There are silences so deep
you can hear
the journeys of the soul,
enormous footsteps
downward in a freezing earth.

ON THE ROAD

It is not good to be poor.
It is good to listen to the wind,

but not when you stand
alone on a road at night
with all your winter parcels,
like a mailbox waiting for
a postman who will never arrive.

The wind comes in carloads,
and goes by with a rushing
of lights and emptiness.

I think only of my home.
I have a pair of slippers for a wife
whose bare feet are waiting.

There is a light through the trees —
it is only a simple place,
with two souls strung together
by nerves and poverty.

It is not good to be poor —
and there are no coins in the wind.

CHRISTMAS, 1962

A soft wind blows
across the islands of anger
and sadness.

The astonished refugee rises
and comes now,
bearing in his white hands
the strange, unshackled
gift of himself.

THE GARDENER

His hoe makes a hush
as of a stone rolled away.

We who are standing here
in rows, green men,
small handfuls of death,

we hardly know this one
who tends us —
dark, inscrutable angel
whose step passes by.

WHAT IS LIFE?

There are no roads
but the paths we make
through sleep and darkness.

An invisible friend: a ghost,
like a black wind
that buffets and steadies
the lost bystander
     who thinks he sees.

INTO THE GLACIER

With the green lamp of the spirit
of sleeping water
taking us by the hand . . .

Deeper and deeper,
a luminous blackness opening
like the wings of a raven —

as though a heavy wind
were rising through all the houses
we ever lived in —

the cold rushing in,
our blankets flying away
into the darkness,
and we, naked and alone,
awakening forever . . .

THE TUNDRA

The tundra is a living
body, warm in the grassy
autumn sun; it gives off
the odor of crushed
blueberries and gunsmoke.

In the tangled lakes
of its eyes a mirror of ice

is forming, where
frozen gut-piles shine
with a dull, rosy light.

Coarse, laughing men
with their women;
one by one the tiny campfires
flaring under the wind.

Full of blood, with a sound
like clicking hoofs,
the heavy tundra slowly
rolls over and sinks
in the darkness.

Part II

THE STONE HARP

1971

THE STONE HARP

A road deepening in the north,
strung with steel,
resonant in the winter evening,
as though the earth were a harp
soon to be struck.

As if a spade
rang in a rock chamber:

in the subterranean light,
glittering with mica,
a figure like a tree turning to stone
stands on its charred roots
and tries to sing.

Now there is all this blood
flowing into the west,
ragged holes at the waterline of the sun—
that ship is sinking.

And the only poet is the wind,
a drifter
who walked in from the coast
with empty pockets.

He stands on the road
at evening, making a sound
like a stone harp
strummed
by a handful of leaves . . .

THE LEMMINGS

No one is pleased with himself
or with others.

No one squeaks gently
or touches a friendly nose.

In this darkness beneath
a calm whiteness
there are growls and scuffles;

the close smell of a neighbor
makes them all dream
of a brown river
swelling toward the sea.

In each small breast
the hated colony disintegrates.

WOLVES

Last night I heard wolves howling,
their voices coming from afar
over the wind-polished ice – so much
brave solitude in that sound.

They are death's snowbound sailors;
they know only a continual
drifting between moonlit islands,
their tongues licking the stars.

But they sing as good seamen should,
and tomorrow the sun will find them,
yawning and blinking
the snow from their eyelashes.

Their voices rang through the frozen
water of my human sleep,
blown by the night wind
with the moon for an icy sail.

ON BANNER DOME

Ten miles from home,
I climbed through the clear
spring sunlight
to an island of melting snow.

Among spilled boulders,
four huts tied in the shape of a cross
tugged at their moorings.

The loosened hand of a door
clapped across the wilderness.
The wind lifted a carton
that raced away like a flailing angel.

In the creaking silence
I heard the effort of a murdered man,
the one left behind,
whose stretched lips torture
the music of resurrection.

The sunlight is never warm
in such a place; to sleep there
is to dream that the ropes
that hold you to earth are letting go,
and around the straining tent
of your life there prowls and sniffs
a fallen black star who overturns
stones and devours the dead.

THE TRAIN STOPS AT HEALY FORK

We pressed our faces
against the freezing glass,
saw the red soil
mixed with snow,
and a strand of barbed wire.

A line of boxcars
stood open on a siding,
their doorways
briefly afire in the sunset.

We saw the scattered iron
and timber of the campsite,
the coal seam
in the river bluff,
the twilight green of the icefall.

But the coppery tribesmen
we looked for had vanished,
the children of wind and shadow,
gone off with their rags
and hunger
to the blue edge of night.

Our train began to move,
bearing north,
sounding its hoarse whistle
in the starry gloom of the canyon.

(1968)

THE RAIN FOREST

A green ape, drinker of clouds,
always thirsty,
always swollen with rain.

His fur matted and dripping,
his face glistening
in patches of watery sunlight;
his eyes are water moving
over grey sand,
peering and drinking.

He shrinks away as night comes,
and the red cedar of dreams
grows in his place
from yellowing roots, its bark
the color of rust and old blood;
dead leaves cling there,
caught in crevices.
Night fills
with the shadowy life of fish
that spawn under sunken logs.

But the green ape always returns;
he stands and watches,
his broad feet clenched in a soil
through which the daylight
seeps and darkens...

Though the ape has not yet spoken,
I listen this evening
to drops of water,
as one might listen
to a tongue growing green.

(1969)

THE CAULIFLOWER

I wanted to be a cauliflower,
all brain and ears,
thinking on the origin of gardens
and the divinity of him
who carefully binds my leaves.

With my blind roots touched
by the songs of the worms,
and my rough throat throbbing
with strange, vegetable sounds,
perhaps I'd feel the parting stroke
of a butterfly's wing . . .

Not like my cousins, the cabbages,
whose heads, tightly folded,
see and hear nothing of this world,
dreaming only on the yellow
and green magnificence
that is hardening within them.

MARIGOLD

This is the plaza of Paradise.
It is always noon,
and the dusty bees are dozing
like pardoned sinners.

TO VERA THOMPSON

(Buried in the Old Military Cemetery at Eagle, Alaska)

Woman whose face
is a blurred map of roots,
I might be buried here
and you dreaming in the warmth
of this late northern summer.

Say I was the last
soldier on the Yukon,
my war fought out
with leaves and thorns.

Here is the field;
it lies thick with horsetail,
fireweed, and stubborn rose.
The wagons and stables
followed the troopers
deep into soil and smoke.
When a summer visitor
steps over the rotting sill
the barracks floor
thumps with a hollow sound.

Life and death grow quieter
and lonelier here by the river.
Summer and winter
the town sleeps and settles,
history is no more than sunlight
on a weathered cross.

The picket fence sinks
to a row of mossy shadows,
the gate locks with a rusty pin.
Stand there now
and say that you loved me,

that I will not be forgotten
when a ghostwind
drifts through the canyon,
and our years grow deep
under snow of these roses and stones.

(1968–81)

CHOOSING A STONE

It grows cold in the forest
of rubble.

There the old hunters survive
and patch their tents with tar.

They light fires in the night
of obsidian –
instead of trees they burn
old bottles and windowpanes.

Instead of axe blows and leaves
falling,
there is always the sound
of moonlight breaking,
of brittle stars ground together.

The talk there is of deadfalls
and pits armed
with splinters of glass,

and of how one chooses a stone.

IN NATURE

Here too are life's victims,
captives of an old umbrella,
lives wrecked
by the lifting of a stone.

Sailors marooned
on the island of a leaf
when their ship
of mud and straw went down.

Explorers lost
among roots and raindrops,
drunkards sleeping it off
in the fields of pollen.

Cities of sand that fall,
dust towers that blow away.
Penal colonies
from which no one returns.

Here too, neighborhoods
in revolt, revengeful columns;
evenings at the broken wall,
black armies in flight . . .

IN THE MIDDLE OF AMERICA

I

In Oberlin the university park
with its trodden snow
and black, Siberian trees:

there were puffs of yellow
smoke in the branches,
sullen flashes
from distant windows.

The hooded figures of partisans
swirled around me,
hauling their weapons
from one bivouac to another.

II

Thereafter on that cold
spring morning
I saw the bird of omen
alight in a thicket.

Like my own heart, a flower
folded in upon itself,
bitterly dreaming,
it wore brightly the color
of blood and rebellion.

III

In the middle of America
I came to an old house
stranded on a wintry hill.

It contained a fire; men and women
of an uncertain generation
gathered before it. The talk
was of border crossings,
mass refusals, flag burnings,
and people who stand or fall.

I moved among them,
I listened and understood.

(1967)

THE SNOWBOUND CITY

I believe in this stalled magnificence,
this churning chaos of traffic,
a beast with broken spine,
its hoarse voice hooded in feathers
and mist; the baffled eyes
wink amber and slowly darken.

Of men and women suddenly walking,
stumbling with little sleighs
in search of Tibetan houses –
dust from a far-off mountain
already whitens their shoulders.

When evening falls in blurred heaps,
a man losing his way among churches
and schoolyards feels under his cold hand
the stone thoughts of that city,

impassable to all but a few children
who went on into the hidden life
of caves and winter fires,
their faces glowing with disaster.

THE SWEATER OF VLADIMIR
USSACHEVSKY

Facing the wind of the avenues
one spring evening in New York,
I wore under my thin jacket
a sweater given me by the wife
of a genial Manchurian.

The warmth in that sweater changed
the indifferent city block by block.
The buildings were mountains
that fled as I approached them.

The traffic became sheep and cattle
milling in muddy pastures.
I could feel around me the large
movements of men and horses.

It was spring in Siberia or Mongolia,
wherever I happened to be.
Rough but honest voices called to me
out of that solitude:
they told me we are all tired
of this coiling weight,
the oppression of a long winter;
that it was time to renew our life,
burn the expired contracts,
elect new governments.

The old Imperial sun has set,
and I must write a poem to the Emperor.
I shall speak it like the man
I should be, an inhabitant of the frontier,
clad in sweat-darkened wool,
my face stained by wind and smoke.

Surely the Emperor and his court
will want to know what a fine
and generous revolution begins tomorrow
in one of his remote provinces . . .

(1967)

GUEVARA

Somewhere inside me,
perhaps under my left shoulder,
there is a country named
Guevara.

I discovered it one day
in October,

when I fell into a cave
which suddenly opened
in my chest.

I found myself climbing
a hill, steep
and slippery with blood.
The ghost of a newspaper
floated before me
like an ashen kite.

I was a long way from the top
when I halted;
I felt something wrong
with my life, like a man
who has marched for years
under an enemy flag.

I came down from that hill
bearing a secret wound;
though a fever beats there,
I still don't know
what I suffered –
a truce with my own darkness,
or some obscure defeat
on the red slope of my heart.

A DREAM OF THE POLICE

I

About the hour the December moon
went down, I awoke to a deep murmur,
looking out through years of sleep
on a snowlit public square.

A crowd of people surged across
that space toward a building
retreating into the distance.

And suddenly blocking their way
rode a force of mounted men
whose helmets and buckles
flashed with a wintry light.

I I

I saw in that glittering distance
a collision of ghosts,
their tangled, deliberate fury —
the flying shadows of fists
and the wiry lightning of whips.

As if all the armored years
were riding, the flanks of the horses
changed into clanging metal,
their legs became churning wheels.
From loose stones rolled underfoot,
traces of white smoke
rose on the cold, still air.

I I I

The people fell back, a field of wheat
pressed darkly under a storm,
and they and the horsemen dispersed
into a grey vagueness of alleys
and windy encampments . . .

There was only a silence,
the empty square, by now a prairie
stretching into the stars,
with a few creeping or frozen bodies,
and a bloodstain turning black
in the snow of my sleep.

THE WAY WE LIVE

Having been whipped through Paradise
and seen humanity
strolling like an overfed beast
set loose from its cage,
a man may long for nothing so much
as a house of snow,
a blue stone for a lamp,
and a skin to cover his head.

THE LEGEND OF PAPER PLATES

They trace their ancestry
back to the forest.
There all the family stood,
proud, bushy and strong.

Until hard times,
when from fire and drought
the patriarchs crashed.

The land was taken for taxes,
the young people cut down
and sold to the mills.

Their manhood and womanhood
was crushed, bleached
with bitter acids,
their fibers dispersed
as sawdust
among ten million offspring.

You see them at any picnic,
at ballgames, at home,
and at state occasions.

They are thin and pliable,
porous and identical.
They are made to be thrown away.

(1969)

DREAM OF THE CARDBOARD LOVER

She fell away from her earthly husband;
it was night in the city
and a dim lamp shone.

The street seemed empty and silent,
but on the pavement before her
lay something weakly flapping.

She bent over and saw in it
the shape of a man, but he
was flattened and thin like a carton.

She picked him up, and looking
into those battered eyes,
she thought she knew him, and cried:

"We sat together in school, long ago,
you were always the one I loved!"

And the cardboard hero shed a paper tear
as he leaned against her
in the dreamlight,
growing dimmer and dimmer.

INSTRUCTIONS TO A SENTRY

You will be standing alone,
leaning toward sundown.
Listen, and mutter
the name of an enemy.

Blown upon by the night wind,
you will change into a tree,
a conifer
holding an armful of ravens.

From a moaning and creaking empire
will come the night messengers,
creatures of claw and fur
whispering words that are leaves
driven before
the immense occupation of winter.

As the sunlit camp slowly retreats
under the tent of a shadow,
remember
how once a demented prophet
described this land:

the horizon where a peach tree
calmly ripened,
how the cow of that wilderness
stood guard
in her thicket of fire.

THE END OF THE STREET

It would be at the end
of a bad winter,
the salty snow turning black,
a few sparrows cheeping

in the ruins of
a dynamited water tower.

The car is out of gas;
someone has gone to look.

Your evening is here.

FOR A YOUNG GIRL

We leaned on a railing
at the small boat harbor
and looked far down.

Our faces floated toward us,
oily and discolored,
mouths and eyes
stretched open on the future.

One after another the years
went by,
vast grey ships of the sun.

The bodies of gulls and whales,
trees, and rotting men,
rolled in the wake.

I saw your face, baffled
and far away, as that smoky water
deepened over your life...

A tide full of sound,
the noise in a cannon shell
held to the ear
of a child growing deaf.

(1967)

DÜRER'S VISION

The country is not named,
but it looks like home.

A scarred pasture,
thick columns of rain,
or smoke . . .

A dark, inverted mushroom
growing from the sky
into the earth.

SMOKE

An animal smelling
of ashes
crossed the hills
that morning.

I closed the door
and windows,
but on the floor
a smoky light
gleamed like old tin.

All day that animal
came and went,
sniffing at trees
still vaguely green,
its fur catching
in the underbrush.

At sundown, it settled
upon the house,
its breath
thick and choking . . .

(1968)

MOONS

There are moons like continents,
diminishing to a white stone
softly smoking
in a fogbound ocean.

Equinoctial moons,
immense rainbarrels spilling
their yellow water.

Moons like eyes turned inward,
hard and bulging
on the blue cheek of eternity.

And moons half-broken,
eaten by eagle shadows . . .

But the moon of the poet
is soiled and scratched, its seas
are flowing with dust.

And other moons are rising,
swollen like boils –

in their bloodshot depths
the warfare of planets
silently drips and festers.

THE MIDDLE AGES

Always on the point of falling asleep,
the figures of men and beasts.

Faces, deeply grained with dirt,
a soiled finger pointing inward.

Like Dürer's Knight, always haunted
by two companions:

the Devil, with a face like a matted hog,
disheveled and split;

and Death, half dog, half monkey,
a withered bishop with an hourglass.

There's a cold lizard underfoot,
the lancehead glitters in its furry collar;

but it's too late now to storm the silence
on God's forbidden mountain.

You have to go on as the century darkens,
the reins still taut in that armored fist.

TO A MAN GOING BLIND

As you face the evenings
coming on steeper and snowier,
and someone you cannot see
reads in a strained voice
from the book of storms . . .

Dreamlike, a jet climbs
above neighboring houses;
the streets smell
of leafsmoke and gasoline.

Summer was more like a curse
or a scar, the accidental blow
from a man of fire
who carelessly turned toward you
and left his handprint glowing
whitely on your forehead.

All the lamps in your home town
will not light the darkness
growing across a landscape
within you; you wait
like a leaning flower, and hear
almost as if it were nothing,
the petrified rumble
from a world going blind.

"IT MUST ALL BE DONE OVER..."

The houses begin to come down,
the yards are deserted,
people have taken to tents
and caravans, like restless cattle
breaking stride,
running off with their wagons
under a rumbling cloud.

There are too many stories,
rumors, and shadows;
like hordes of grasshoppers
they eat up the land,
columns of brutal strangers.

I leave my house to the wind
without baggage or bitterness;

I must make my life into
an endless camp,
learn to build with air,
water, and smoke...

(1969)

THE TURNING

I

A bear loped before me
on a narrow, wooded road;
with a sound like a sudden
shifting of ashes, he turned
and plunged into his own blackness.

I I

I keep a fire and tell a story:
I was born one winter
in a cave at the foot of a tree.

The wind thawing in a northern
forest opened a leafy road.

As I walked there, I heard
the tall sun burning its dead;
I turned and saw behind me
a charred companion,
my shed life.

CRANES

That vast wheel turning
in the sky,
turning and turning
on the axle of the sun . . .

The wild cries,
the passionate wingbeat,
as the creaking
helm of the summer
comes round,

and the laboring ship
plunges on . . .

THE FLIGHT

It may happen again – this much
I can always believe
when our dawn fills with frightened neighbors
and the ancient car refuses to start.

The gunfire of locks and shutters
echoes next door to the house
left open
for the troops that are certain to come.

We shall leave behind nothing but cemeteries,

and our life like a refugee cart
overturned in the road,
a wheel slowly spinning . . .

Part III

TWENTY POEMS

1971

THE PITCHER OF MILK

Today is the peace of this mist
and its animals, as if all
the cows and goats in the land
gave milk to the dawn.

The same mist that rises
from battlefields, out of the mouths
and eye-sockets of horse
and man, it mingles with smoke
from moss fires
in the homesteader's clearing.

I and the others come to the doors
of cold houses, called
by the thin ringing of a spoon;

we stand with our brimming bowls,
called to where Peace awakens
in a cloud of white blood.

A WINTER LIGHT

We still go about our lives
in shadow, pouring the white cup full
with a hand half in darkness.

Paring potatoes, our heads
bent over a dream—
glazed windows through which
the long, yellow sundown looks.

By candle or firelight
your face still holds
a mystery that once
filled caves with the color
of unforgettable beasts.

THE INVADERS

It was the country I loved,
and they came over the hills
at daybreak.
          Their armor
hoisted a dirty flag to the dawn,
the cold air
glittered with harsh commands.

Up and down the roads of Alaska,
the clanging bootsoles,
the steely clatter of wheels,

treading down forests, bruising
the snows —
          bringing
the blossom of an angry sundown,

their cannon and blue flares
pumping fear into the night.

THE MAN WHO SKINS ANIMALS

I

He comes down from the hill
just at dusk, with a faint
clinking of chains.

He speaks to no one, and when
he sits down by the fire
his eyes, staring into the
shadows, have a light like drops
of blood in the snow.

I I

There is a small, soft thing
in the snow, and its ears
are beginning to freeze.

Its eyes are bright, but
what they see is not this world
but some other place
where the wind, warm
and well fed, sleeps
on a deep, calm water.

THE HERMITAGE

In the forest below the stairs
I have a secret home,
my name is carved in the roots.

I own a crevice stuffed with moss
and a couch of lemming fur;
I sit and listen to the music
of water dripping on a distant stone,
or I sing to myself
of stealth and loneliness.

No one comes to see me,
but I hear outside
the scratching of claws,
the warm, inquisitive breath . . .

And once in a strange silence
I felt quite close
the beating of a human heart.

THE GOSHAWK

I will not walk on that road again,
it is like a story one hesitates to begin.

I found myself alone,
the fur close around my face, my feet
soft and quiet in the frost.

Then, with a cold, rushing sound,
came a shadow like the death-angel
with buffeting wings,
his talons gripping my shoulder,
the bright beak tearing and sinking . . .

Then, then I was falling, swept
into the deepening red sack of a voice:

"Little rabbit, you are bleeding again;
with his old fire-born passion
the Goshawk feeds on your timid heart."

IMAGES OF THE FROST KING

Once he stood at the door
like a birch unraveling in the wind.

He pounded the ice in his chest,
and his eyes were cold with grandeur.

In a mirror held by the forest
a cloud of aspens
leans upon a deserted throne.

The Frost King is sleeping,
his face darkened
by the flight of nocturnal thrushes.

THE SUDDEN SPRING

The coyote had just spoken
and lay down to rest in a snowdrift.

March, like a fly awakened too early,
droned between somnolence
and a furious boredom.

No one remembered the autumnal
prophet, teller of drowsy stories
to be continued . . .

Winter, the unfinished, the abandoned,
slumped like a mourner
between two weeping candles.

LARKSPUR

The blue giant is passing,
king of this field.

His trumpets blow pure cobalt,
he brings with him
audiences of the deepest indigo.

By his command
the sky-stained meadows overflow,
and bridges of azure
stretch far into evening . . .

where the king, his train halted,
stands alone in his blueness.

STONES

They are dreaming existence.
One is a man, and one
is a woman. Beside them an animal,

someone who followed them
into the distance
until their feet grew heavy
and sank in the soil.

And the life within them became
an expanding shadow,
a blue gravel on which they fed
as they changed;

standing there so solid and dark,
as if they were waiting
for God to remember their names.

THE MUSHROOM GROVE

Here the forest people
died of a sexual longing.

The ground trampled in their passion
healed into a cemetery,
with a few flowers
like frayed parachutes.

Their headstones are umbrellas,
black and weeping.

THE INSECTS

Maggots, wrinkled white men
building a temple of slime.

Green blaze of the blowfly
that lights the labor of corpses.

The carrion beetle awakening
in a tunnel of drying flesh
like a miner surprised by the sun.

And rolling his bronze image
into the summer, the scarab,
whose armor shone once
in a darkness called Egypt.

THE DANCE

for George Hitchcock

The red armchair is empty.
The man who sat there
is turning in the room,
holding in his hands
a painted jungle.

The faces of his audience,
at first like flowers,
pale from lack of sunlight,
begin to darken
and put on the look
of watchers in a clearing.

No sound but a stealthy
scratching, and the slow steps
turning against smoke
and silence, as the dance

gathers everything
into a haunted forest . . .

From the bark of those trees
sprout flowers
like drops of blood,
and birds' heads
of a threatening blue.

(1967)

RYDER

The moonlight has touched them all . . .

The dream hulk with its hollows
driven black,
the ancient helmsman, his handbones
glinting with salt and memory.

Under the sail of sleep, torn and flapping,
night's crowded whale broaches,
heaving another Jonah
to the shoal of a broken world.

Jehovah's arm outstretched
like a locust cloud at sea,

and the moon itself,
a pale horse of torment flying . . .

PAUL KLEE

The hot mice feeding in red,
the angry child
clutching a blue watermelon –
these are the sun and moon.

The Tunisian patch,
where beneath some crooked
black sticks
a woman's face is burning.

There are also disasters at sea,
compasses gone wrong –

only because of a gentle
submarine laughter,
no one is drowning.

(1969)

SPILLED MILK

When I see milk spilled on the table,
another glass overturned,
I think of all the cows who labor in vain.

So many tons of forage spent,
so many udders filling and emptying,
forest after forest
stripped for paper cartons,
the wax from millions of candles melting...

A broad sheet of milk spills across
the tables of the world,
and this child stands
with a sopping sponge in his hand,
saying he never meant to do it.

(1970)

SLEEP

Whether we fall asleep under the moon
like gypsies, with silver coins
in our pockets, or crawl deep
into a cave through which the warm,
furry bats go grinning and flying,
or put on a great black coat
and simply ride away into the darkness,

we become at last like trees
who stand within themselves, thinking.

And when we awake – if we do –
we come back bringing the images
of a lonely childhood: the hands
we held, the threads we unwound
from the shadows beneath us;
and sounds as of voices in another room
where some part of our life
was being prepared – near which we lay,
waiting for our life to begin.

Part IV

INTERIM

UNCOLLECTED POEMS

FROM THE 1970S

THE OREGON COAST

I

This half-ruined porch of giants,
rough men of granite and basalt
grown hairy with hemlock and fur.

They sit looking down through storms,
forming some dark, volcanic thought,
their only speech the sound of waves
crashing against their knees.

The green pillars of their temple
topple behind them; sunlight
leans on the sprawled columns,
and sheep crop the gutted floors.

I I

The centuries unroll in free-falling
loops of stone. Now and then a giant
pitches from his loosened chair,
the ocean grows heavy with evening,
night closes the small white look
of alders among the ferns.

Long after, in the leveled wreck
of California,
I remembered the inward sweep
of a granite forehead, the drenched
magnificence not yet destroyed.

(1970)

PANORAMA

The games of beasts and children,
locked antlers, crossed swords
and clanging shields;
the man-killing stone loosed

from the sling, these boyish shouts
and the warning clamor of geese . . .

All pass before the sentry
with his toy pistol cocked,
to the camp in seclusion
behind the sleeping hill.

It's the sound that passion makes,
this hand stroking a breast,
pulling a turnip from stubborn soil,
cracking a bone, driving a nail;
and the same hand reaches
through steel to touch the stars.

While we guard against thieves
for the acorn deep in a burrow
or the coin held close in our pocket,
we are scared by the flurry
of wings in a thicket, and flinch
from the anger of sparrows.

We turn one ear to the flight of missiles,
listen earthward with the other
for fieldmice squeaking in the grass.

It is the full and divided nature
of things, violent and generous,
cunning and naive,
stalking and lying at rest,
that gives and takes away.

The lion whose sunburnt shoulder
reddens as he turns from repose
at sundown, now to be a hunter,
not a king on the shelf.

(1971)

THE GIRL WHO BURIED SNAKES
IN A JAR

She came to see the bones
whiten in a summer,
and one year later a narrow
mummy with a dusty skin
and flaking scales
would break apart in her hand.

She wanted to see if sunlight
still glinted in those eyes,
to know what it lighted
from a window on the mallow roots,
leaf mold and fallen casques.

And to ask if a single tongue,
one forked flicker in the dark,
had found any heat in death:
in the closed space and chill
of that burial, what speech,
what sign would there be.

She who walked in the canyon early,
parted the grass and halted
upon the living snake, coiled
and mottled by a bitter pool,

unearthed her jar in another spring,
to find the snake spirit gone,
only a little green water standing,
some dust, or a smell.

(1974)

GREEN PIANO

Her hands on the green piano
were sudden and sharp, thin bones
of a bird treading the keys;

and the tune they plucked
came through a throat of wires,
as a wind in bare trees.

She searched that melody harsher
and deeper, hunting downward
among slashes of sunlight,
furrows stricken with shadow,
her fingernails stabbing the earth.

Ponderous and slow, the ivory
and black tongues of an elephant
gave life to a soul of wood.

And the music soared, scale
upon scale, into a dazzling cloud,
a high and furious clapping that broke,

came down as thunder, and stopped
in a waste of echoing rock.

(1973)

TAR

I
A tar baby was born among us,
clutching everything
to its sticky breast.

It awakened one night
in its cradle of asphalt,

bellowed and strained
to get at the world;

then its black heart burst,
thick blood leaked into
the gutters, and its lungs
blew squalor and death.

 I I
Wherever we walk on earth
bits of tar
cling to our footsoles.

Our children are born
with glittering faces,
even our kisses
are stained with petroleum.

Over the seas,
with their mottled islands
and iridescent whales,
a black hand wrinkles in the wind.

(1975)

BECOMING A CROW

The beak will grow
from your mouth and chin,
and your eyes slip away
to the sides of your head;

your fingertips long and feathery,
unable to hold,
your feet naked and grasping.

And all the great words
will stick in your throat,
mere caws and whistles.

You'll be alone in the air,
with the world always
sliding and upside down –
see the continents askew,
all the tilted nations.

And someone standing in a field
below, waving arms of straw:

"Look, look at the crow!"

Black tatters in a world of sticks.

(1973)

LIFE IN AN ASHTRAY

In our thin white paper skins
and freckled collars,
little brown shreds for bones,

we begin with our feet in ashes,
shaking our shoes
in a crazy, crippling dance;

then skate along the glassy
metal rim of our world,
to lean there, sour and reeking...

the only people born tall,
who shrink as they grow.

Prodded by hired matches,
we'd like to complain,

but all our efforts to speak
dissolve in smoke
and gales of coughing.

The yellow glare in our eyes
turning red as we age,
stomping our feet to put out the fire;

and always the old ones crumpling,
crushed from above
by enormous hands,

the young ones beginning to burn.

(1970)

THE BILLBOARDS IN EXILE

I
The truth was finally written,
law came to the billboards.

They were stripped of their promises,
uprooted, and made to walk –
a shabby band of discards
driven as domestic scrap
into the wastes of soap and tin.

II
I will be a weathervane, said one.
And I a water-tower.
And I a mirror.
And I will be a window.
And I a tree...
The big boards creaked in memory.

Each of them looked back
to see again the vanished colors
of their country;
the rich and coppery gleam
of the fortunate,
the charm, the easy pastoral
of manhood and smoke.

I I I
The prayer of the billboards:

Let some hand restore us,
to be in this world
memorial and gesture.

Great artifice of the sun,
give us back our slogans,
our islands of thirst.

Whoever comes this way
with matchbox and flint
to light his bonfire,

let him read in us
of the paradise defaulted
and the vision tamed.

(1977)

THE AUTUMN OF MONEY

Now the slow shrinking of coins,
the dulling of silver, intrusions
of copper and baser metal;

the dates and the mottoes
rubbed off, the profiles smeared,
nickels out of round,
half-dollars shaved to a quarter.

And the greenbacks losing color,
shaking loose in the wind
from the bank doors closing.

Drifts of bills, windrows of checks,
heaps of cash in the gutters;

blazing in weedy lots,
drums of the currency burning.

The needy folk holding their hands
to a brief charity in fire,
for the great wealth and plenty
changed to this scarcity
bleached and blowing, chased
by children with rickety rakes,
stuffing their leafbags full,

for a loaf, for an egg, or a wing.

But now the sour smoke of savings,
wallets and purses gaping
in the panic of wrinkling faces . . .

It is the autumn of money.
The paper grows thin and thinner.
It is ash, it is air,
then nothing, nothing at all.

(1 9 7 1)

TO LIVE AMONG CHILDREN

To live among children,
to listen, an ear to their trouble;
the voices, demanding or gentle,
small hands plucking
the threads of a sleeve:

ask to be told once more
a story repeated by the shadows
looming at cribside.

And what had those shadows to say –
vague and nodding,

dense with the mystery always
towering in the distance?

That little has changed
since that hour we too listened
to a voice speaking in the oak leaves.

And think of the answers we give:

Why the continents drift,
what wind carves the rock
into cities, or blows the people
on their polar journeys;

what legendary shoulder continues
to hold up the sky,
or why the mountain train
never seems to end.

All of our history come to that moment
when we look
at a shadow flying past:

What bird, what beast was that?

(1975)

MUSHROOM FABLE

I knew them all in that age of saliva.

Soapy Tricholoma I knew,
and *Blackening Russula.*
I called *Oak-loving Collybia*
my friend, I gave her
Pig's Ears and *Witches Butter.*

Born a *Smoky Woodlover,* I scored
with *Chicken-in-the-Woods,*

and cast my spawn in a *Fairy Ring.*
I wanted *Dark-Centered Hebeloma*
once, but never found her.

But I turned my back on those
tragic sisters, the *False Morels;*
I pitied the pale *Amanitas*
their bitter names
and bad complexions,
for they were beneath me.

Coral and lichen grew red
and green in my beard;
I wore cap, veil, and ring
when in the shadow of ink
I paid my respects to *King Boletus*
and bowed to his dark applause.

But it is not with them I seek
my reckoning now, in this hour
of betrayals, when mushroom hunters
are aging, and all umbrellas
are ribs and tatters . . .

But with you! O *Bitter False Paxillus!*
With you, *Fat Pholiota!*
With you, *Blushing Inocybe!*
And with you, *Autumnal Galerina!*

To you I come as *Destroying Angel,*
your yellowing *Panther;*
I bring you word of the *Death Cup*
broken – this gray, freezing milk
spilled over churchyards,
meadows and woods . . .

When you rise again you will not
forget the wind that scattered

your flyblown children, or who it was
that sent your names to that region
where *Slime Mold* calms the dead
with Hemlock and Nightshade.

(1972)

IN FIVE YEARS' TIME

In five years' time
our faces may be a map
of roots printed
in the shade of a wall.

Or this: the armor of things
will have fallen,
those who now resemble
alligators and gars
will be sleek in fur.

Or else in the slime
a sleeping engine wakes:
all the ooze and the bubbles
will burst, and the hat
of the forest fly off.

In five years' time,
torn from the fiery
bubble of ourselves,
we may all be walking
in heaven,
battered and dreaming,
our shoes in our hands:

"Where did we come from?
How did it happen?"

Over the cuckoo-land
of our seeming-to-be,
a brief rumble passes
like a cloud:

This story of things
that never happened.

(1975)

LIKE A WAVE

I looked at her face until
I could not see it anymore;
in its place a stormy light
burned on an arm of water.

And so her body, fallen upon
a hillside, thighs overgrown
with thorns and grass,
changed to another country.

Thereafter I loved her
in the smoke of the sunrise,
in every snowfall,
rain and the drift of leaves.

Our lives met in the rift
where earth and sky mingle,
a ground confused in blood;

the upwelling of water
into clouds, lightning over
the plowed furrows, night
and the clearing after.

She spoke to me in the wind,
her words parting the grass
and sea, like a wave
or a running whisper.

(1974)

THE PRESENCE

Out of her sleeping body
(she whom I slept beside)
a figure rose, half of darkness,
an insect of fire in her hair.

As a great moth of phosphor
it floated toward the window,
stayed there against the starlight,
and a hand from the shadowy floor
came and stroked the fire.

Like a coal blown upon, yellow
and a deeper red, it burned above me
in that room. A hand and face
feeding each other's fire
slowly consumed themselves.

A glowing ghost stayed there
combing the ash in her hair,
until the grey light grew
and I awoke.

(1973)

SHAVER

The back door swung open
and our bird flew out,
into the rain
in the cold Thanksgiving morning.

Everyone called and searched
the trees and wires,
or thought of a nook in the eaves
where a tiny knot
of the rainbow might cling
in the dark to come.

But nothing answered out there,
nothing came fluttering
wet to the sill.
The children stopped looking,

and the cage on the shelf
surrounded a stillness
in its seeds and crumbs,
in the wire
of its beak-chipped bars.

(1973)

RAIN

We found some truth in the wet wood
we gathered and burned,
in the smoke that followed us
into the drying fields,
our pieces of flame-bitten candle,
our few books thumbed
until we stopped reading forever.

Our words meant to build bridges
one evening gave way
in the ash of our roots' fire.

I stand with a cloud behind me,
a rolled umbrella in my hand.
You are gone into that grey
emptiness crowded eastward,
and our house is a raft of shingles
sunk under leaves and vines.

(1974)

YETI

I

Our years are driven wild,
and the fear-changed mind
of the people turns once again
to its brute solace —
the night-coursing of monsters,
emblems of blood,
in the sleep of reason.

How often has the stalled
mountaineer awakened,
to hear far down the moonlit
col, the snow-filled cry
of a beast that mates
once in a hundred years.

Out of its cage of sleep
a maimed and shaggy captive
climbs shelf by shelf
and ridge by ridge to a cave
warmed in the icefields,
stuck with hair
and stained with blood.

I I
In this world we think we know,
something will always
be hidden, whether a fern-rib
traced in the oldest rock,

or a force behind our face,
like the pulse of a reptile,
dim and electric.

A possibility we hadn't
thought of, too tall
and thick to be believed.

Its face like a wise ape
driven to the snows,
turns at the starry ford,
gives back one burning
look, and goes.

(1976–91)

TREES ARE PEOPLE AND
THE PEOPLE ARE TREES

And there in the crowded commons
three hundred striding people,
gesturing, eating the air,
halted around us, suddenly quiet.

They sprouted leaves and cones,
they wore strange bark for clothing,
and gently lifted their arms.

(1975)

Part V

CICADA

1977

CICADA

I

I sank past bitten leaves,
tuning in a shell my song
of the absent and deaf.

And that pain came alive
in the dark, shot
with the torment of seeds,
root-ends and wiry elbows.

I I

A whisper, dry and insane,
repeating like a paper drum
something I was,
something I might become:

a little green knife
slitting the wind upstairs,
or a husk in the sod.

I I I

It was late summer
in the grass overhead.
I wanted wings and a voice,

my own tree to climb,
and someone else to answer,
clear across
loud acres of sun.

(1974)

THE INCURABLE HOME

Then I came to the house of wood
and knocked with a cold hand.
My bones shone in my flesh
as the ribs in a paper lantern,
the gold ring slipped from my finger.

The door swung open, strong hands
seized me out of the darkness
and laid me in a bed of wood;
it was heavy, weighted with shadows,
lined with cloth woven from wheat straw.

Four posts stood by the corners;
thick candles were lighted upon them,
and the flames floated
in pools of forest water.
The air smelled of damp leaves and ashes.

People whose faces I knew and had forgotten
wound a chain about my hands.
They dipped their fingers in the water,
wrote their names on a clay tablet
and stood aside,
talking in the far country of sleep.

(1972)

SKAGWAY

I dreamed that I married
and lived in a house in Skagway.

My wife was a tall, strong girl
from the harbor,
her dark hair smelled of rain,

our children walked to school
against the wind.

Through years piled up like boxcars
at a vacant station, my hammer
echoed on the upper floors,
my axe rang in a yard
where leaves and ladders fall.

By kerosene light I wrote
the history of roundhouse rust,
of stalled engines, and cordwood
sinking by the tracks.
Against the October darkness
I set a row of pale
green bottles in a wall
to see the winter sun.

A snowman knocked at night,
he roamed the lots and whispered
through the graveyard fences.

I met in April an aging pioneer
come back for one more summer.
We listened together as
the last excursion
rumbled toward White Pass.

And slowly that fall the houses
grew blank and silent,
the school door shackled with a chain.
My people on an icy barge
turned south, grey gulls in a mist.

I walked down the littered alleys,
searching the lights of broken windows;
with a weathered shingle
I traced in the gravel of Main Street
a map of my fading country . . .

Until my shoes wore out
and I stood alone
with all the Skagway houses,
a ledger in the wind,
my seventy pages peeling.

(1970)

THE MIRROR

I

From the bed where I lay
I saw a tilted mirror
holding together four thin blue
walls and a yellow ceiling.

I I

A door turned its white face
inward; I rose and stood before
a rain-streaked window
whose paper curtains whispered
against me in the cloudy light.

I I I

I went farther and deeper
into that world of glass,
prowling an endless hallway
where lonely coathangers
banged softly together.

I V

Down the turning stairway
under a lamp suddenly dark
I came to an entry, or an exit;
and beyond that I saw the grey
siding of the roominghouse,
a sign blowing and creaking . . .

V
Tarpaper and wind,
a street rolling stones
to the foot of a snowy mountain.

(1970)

POEM ABOUT BIRCH TREES

From the life held back in secret,
a hand with many fingers
questions the blind face that is Nature.

Those leaves shed rain from the soul,
yet each is a torch set afire
by the sun; so the young tree
dreams of one match for the world.

But too long withheld, the heartwood
sours and slowly rots; the tree
totters within, though its white bark
shines and seems to hold.

Until one day, just a little wind
on a load of snow,
and that hollow life breaks down.

(1971)

THE STONE BEAR

I
An old, root-crowded cemetery
near Dyea, Alaska. Among
the devil's-club and ferns,
I found a stone bear
on the pedestal of a grave.

In that body of rusty wire
and crumbling mortar,
it stood and clawed the air.

I I

Slow pulse in a den of roots,
remember a grey shadow world
blowing in drifts overhead,
windfall and creaking timber.

Dream and childhood wintered alone,
to nourish a belly of ants
and stare through fences
at the hostile fields reeking
with strange, forbidden meat.

I was hunted by a moving fire,
trailed by bloodlight in the snow.
Captivity, a noose of wire,
made secretly inside a cage
hatred of dogs and men with chains.

A snout of quills, a paw that burns;
this hurt and hungry beast,
disconsolate and dancing
among the devil's-club and ferns.

I I I

I left the graveyard by a chosen path,
carrying in myself an aging strength.
Out of the forest, by sunlight
and rain, footbound to the soil,
a doomed and singing spirit.

Before me the unclimbed summit
of my life, the rock where
I may stand in the biting air
of another, far-off October.

There in a wind spilling down
from wintry pastures,
I'll pull my fur around me
and freeze into living stone.

(1972)

GOODBYE TO THE FLOWERCLOCK

The hour belonged to hemlock
and nightshade; all around me
the dayflowers perished,
the garden I planted in my flesh
and watered with my blood.

The hour was wound tight
under the bark of the birch tree,
in the ice of the streambed,
and lay like an iron shadow
on the sundial I wore as a heart.

It was time to push away
the four walls of the years,
to go to the end of the path
and go beyond...

The flowerclock whirled
in the darkness, all its petals
flew off, and the stem
swung hollow and broken
like a blade of straw.

(1969)

MEN AGAINST THE SKY

Across the Oregon plateau
I saw strange man-figures
made up from rivets and girders,
harnessed with cables;

tall, electric, burning
in the strong evening light,
they marched into the sunset.

Their outstretched arms were bearing
away the life of that country . . .

A scorched silence fell over
the shadowy red buttes,
and sank forever
in a town with one long street.

They left behind the smell
of sagebrush mixed with ashes,
black bands of cattle
quietly drifting;

a dry lake filling with moonlight,
and one old windmill,
its broken arms
clattering in the darkness.

(1969)

DUSK OF THE REVOLUTIONARIES

Now we shall learn to live in the dark;
we have gone past
the last military household,
camped here in the wind
blowing sparks and ashes away
down the cold night country.

We were serious, back there
under the barracks,
loving the smell of gunpowder,
and dreamed of bringing to earth
the towering
decrepitude of life.

Our hunted names spoken with care
by the few strange youths
who remember,

history for us becomes
the dark side of a mountain,
as the great cloud-utopias
burn out in the west.

(1969)

THERE ARE NO SUCH TREES
IN ALPINE, CALIFORNIA

I wanted a house
on the shore of Summer Lake,
where the cottonwoods burn
in a stillness beyond October,
their fires warming the Oregon farms.

There John Fremont and his men
rested when they came down late
from the winter plateau,
and mended in the waning sunlight.

Sprawled among frayed tents
and balky campfires, they told
of their fellowship in fever,
stories torn from buffalo tongues,
words of wind in a marrowbone;
how the scorched flower of the prairie
came to ash on a shore of salt.

Then silent and half asleep,
they gazed through green smoke
at the cottonwoods, spent leaves
caught fire and falling,
gathering more light and warmth
from the hearth of the sun,
climbing and burning again.

And there I too wanted to stay . . .
speak quietly to the trees,
tell in a notebook sewn from
their leaves my brief of passage:
long life without answering speech,
grief enforced in that absence;
much joy in the weather,
spilled blood on the snow.

With a few split boards,
a handful of straightened nails,
a rake and a broom;
my chair by the handmade window,
the stilled heart come home
through smoke and falling leaves.

(1 9 7 0)

THE TREE THAT BECAME A HOUSE

They came to live in me
who never lived in the woods before.

They kindled a fire
in my roots and branches,
held out their hands
never cramped by the weight of an axe.

The flames lighted a clearing
in the dark overhead, a sky of wood;

they burned in me a little hollow
like a moon of ash.

I stand here fastened in a living box,
half in my dream life
with finches, wind and fog –

an endless swaying,
divided in the walls that keep them,
in the floors that hold them up,
in the sills they lean upon.

The children look out in wonder
at trees shouldering
black against the starlight;
they speak in whispers,
searching the forest of sleep.

My split heart creaks in the night
around them,
my dead cones drop in silence.

(1971)

LEAVES AND ASHES

Standing where the city and the forest
were walled together,
she dreamed intently on a stone.

A passage cut in its granite face
told of the sea at morning,
how a hand grew steady in its depth.

Then a cold wind blew through the oaks;
the leaves at her feet got up
like startled children, whirled
and fled along the wintry ground.

In the soil a jar of ashes
settled and slept.

It was at the end of a steep
and bitter decade, in a year of burials,
of houses sold, the life they held
given away for the darkness to keep.

She stood alone in the windy arbor,
the tall brown house of November
slowly unbuilding around her.

(1969)

THE WHISTLE COLUMN

On a hill above the town
where we all were born,
I stood by a slender column,
drummed my fingers
on the cold blue stone.

My people gathered around me;
I said to them: "Listen! . . . "
and pressed the column
between my hands. Piercing
and sad, the noon whistle
blew in the town below.

I looked for a crank,
a rod of blackened iron
bent in a foundry fire,
sure if I wound it up,
the column would blow
again and again.

My audience drifted away
in that light, whether dawn
or evening I couldn't tell.

I held one child by the shoulder,
I said to him: "Listen!..."
and firmly squeezed his hand.

From the stone and bricks
of our town, from the cars,
the clocks and the steeples,
a far away sound began,
every horn, every bell.

(1971)

PETER'S START

See the house
with the Christmas tree,
see the paper and string.

Now see the door open,
see the boy leave,
watch the door bang
as it closes.

See the tree shake in the wind,
see the family talking,
the mother pointing,
the father shouting—

See the good house.

See the clouds blacken,
the rain coming down;
see the lightning,
imagine the thunder!...

Mad, that's what the father was.

See the darkness,
see the light,
see the tree broken,
the boy asleep in its branches.

See the door standing up
by itself when the storm
blew the house away.

(1971)

THE RAIN GLASS

A winter morning, and the sea
breaks on the harbor wall.

Rain moves up the lonely street
under swaying wires,
blowing across the empty playground;
the air smells
of metal, kelp, and tar.

I hear the thrashing of leaves
against these windows;
the house is cold,
but the shifting glare of a fire
shines on wet asphalt.

Chairs, forms of silent people;
faces blurred in the clouding
of many small mirrors.

I wait in the doorway of a room
with grey walls and distant pictures.

(1971)

JANE'S DREAM

All in a waking fever
she came to a room she knew
and opened the door.

A room without fire or light,
still forms of her children
lay close on the floor.

She spoke and no one answered.
Bending, she touched them
one by one, their bodies and faces.

Found one whose throat was torn –
blood on her hands,
blood wet on the floor.

"There was a stranger . . ."
"We didn't want to tell."
"Mother mustn't know."
"Don't say a word."

All lying still in the darkness.

(1972)

THE CHASE

Once man chased his woman through
the woods. He caught a glimpse of her
wetness beneath a waterfall, and sucked
his breath. She was a smell in the night,
a dumb presence under thatch, warming
the mouth of a cave with sticks, until
he closed with her in the underbrush.
    Now through the rooms of his household
he still pursues her. He catches sight
of her over the morning paper, touches

her sometimes in the intervals of an
argument. He knows her presence in his
children, her distance by day.

    Evening after evening he runs her
to earth, until they both lie panting
in that darkness made equally of night
and themselves.

(1 9 7 1)

THE WHALE IN THE BLUE
WASHING MACHINE

There are depths in a household
where a whale can live . . .

His warm bulk swims from room
to room, floating by on the stairway,
searching the drafts, the cold
currents that lap at the sills.

He comes to the surface hungry,
sniffs at the table,
and sinks, his wake rocking the chairs.

His pulsebeat sounds at night
when the washer spins, and the dryer
clanks on stray buttons . . .

Alone in the kitchen darkness,
looking through steamy windows
at the streets draining away in fog;

watching and listening,
for the wail of an unchained buoy,
the steep fall of his wave.

(1 9 7 1)

RED TREES IN THE WIND

This burning flight of summer,
a forest of leaves going by up the street,
one leaf and another,
thin and frantic butterflies
with red wings on their shoulders.

In this neighborhood where life
is all roots and branches,
I plant trees by day, and listen
toward evening for rustling armies,
rolling cans, burst watermains.

I dream, then wake and search
for the woman beside me
with these hands that turn and catch
in the sleeplessness of too early autumn.

I see in the glowing darkness
a man standing alone on the sidewalk,
his red skin and burning clothes;
he cries aloud in the wind:
"This world shall come to nothing!"

And there is no one to hear or believe.

(1971)

THE WEAVER

for Blair

By a window in the west
where the orange light falls,
a girl sits weaving in silence.

She picks up threads of sunlight,
thin strands from the blind shadows

fallen to the floor,
as her slim hands swiftly pass
through cords of her loom.

Light from a wine glass
goes into the weave,
light passing from the faces
of those who watch her;
now the grey flash from a mirror
darkening against the wall.

And her batten comes down,
softly beating the threads,
a sound that goes and comes again,
weaving this house and the dusk
into one seamless, deepening cloth.

(1971)

THE CALENDAR

Let this book as it ends
remember the hand that wrote it,
the eye that slowly
learned its alphabet,
the thumb that peeled back its pages.

The days were marked beforehand:
phases of the moon,
a flight to Pennsylvania,
the changing birthdays of children.

Words, ciphers on paper,
paper that curls and yellows:
Valentines, Easters,
a lot of numbers to throw away...

Something about a year
dying in anger,
something about starlight and sleep.

(1972)

FOR ANNE, AT A LITTLE DISTANCE

Thinking of you, of your letters,
your name, your sunlight,
and the oak bough that spoke once
so strangely in your dream . . .

I see your child's drawings
pinned to my wall—
always the lion's head and mane,
some common word misspelled,
an old rancor and confusion
come here to speak on the page.

The rounding figure of a girl,
slowly realizing out of household
discord, tumult of playgrounds,
the insect murmur of classrooms,
body and spirit of a woman.

Beyond the poverty of this time,
this crime of relentless clocks,
a far sound comes nearer:
shade trees raining metal, houses
gone under a vengeful shadow . . .

I remember a day at Pool Rock,
the blue vein deep in your throat,
the wind on the mountain
that almost carried you away.

(1974)

JONNA

The depth of the evening
sank blue in your eyes.
I have never seen a mountain
so small, never watched
in so clear a window
a forest, a sky, and a rock.

Your birch trees stood aside
in their scattered whiteness,
saying something the spruces
in their darkness couldn't hear;
yet all trees swayed together
in the same interior wind.

With a hand and a whisper
we might have seized that instant,
held back the twilight;
let mountain and sky make a calm,
not distant and cold,
but there with us in that room.

But a voice speaking from a throat
in the dusk at our feet
made the evening vaster and deeper:
the cry of someone standing alone
at the far rim of the earth,
gone dark and silent in a wink.

(1973)

DAPHNE

I

Of yourself and your beginnings,
these scattered images
say what you are
and what you may become.

Morning, and Spring come again
to the island where you live,
always Daphne. Soul of the wind,

there are vines at your throat,
your ear thinned to a shell
that listens to water and the voice
of a sea bird crying in the fog.

I I
I know three women that are you:

One keeps track of the silver
in a box of drawers, she loves
the glitter and the falling sound.

Another climbs all day the rooms
in a vacant house; she rocks
at night before a fire, reads
from a large red book, withheld
and alone.
             And the third
calls music from a heart of wood.

I I I
You rise from your sleep
as from a lover gone silent and cold.
You walk in a sunken green light,
stand before your water mirror,
then cut off your hair.

I find you, I lose you. You change,
stand fast in a makeshift of shadows;
you leave, and ferry my heart away.

Your voice from its inner distance
saying your poem, your myth,
born from the bark of your tree.

(1974)

CHANGES

You are not that Daphne
spoken of in whispers,
your firelit leaves
blowing a thousand years.

And I am not that Apollo
pursuing forever a sandal trace,
or the voice of a bird
retreating always deeper
into the gloom of the household elms.

But something clings to you
like a wrinkled vine,
or the shadow on a stone
grown chill with the absence
of someone who has
a better thing to do.

What I meet is air,
a trace of lilac in a hallway,
a smear of blood on a leaf.

Standing too long in this doorway,
I will change to a dry stick
planted here,
a rack for all who walk in pain,
a cane for the blind and the halt.

(1974)

THE TUNNEL

Disappearance begins with you,
always ready to turn,
seeking a change,
a mask, a face not your own,

a hollow filled with roots
and angry sighs.

You leave at an inner distance
a shadow, or the shell
of a shadow,
standing, sleeping beside me.

All the landmarks drained
by the wind of your passing –
fields and rivers, streets
I do not know, your name itself . . .

Your face a tunnel of lights
which I no longer see.

(1974)

FOR DAPHNE AT LONE LAKE

From the window of your sister's house
you can see lake water
foaming under the evening wind,
a cloudy light through the willow
shorn of leaves,
and the heron on the landing.

Turn and speak to yourself
of the few other things you know,
whatever can still be touched
within you:

Not a chair turned to the fire,
nor the leaf-pattern lighting a wall,
nor the silver pitcher
signed in your grandmother's time,
worn thin by your hand;
these things will be melted down,
charred in the fire to come.

Speak of your heart
burned to a seed of ash,
and love, a small white stone
gleaming in the shallows.

A few words spoken into the darkness,
a spirit in the wind,
the rattle of a few dry leaves
on a basement wall . . .

The cry of the heron, suddenly stilled
as it flies from the landing
over this cold lake at evening.

(1974)

BRAND

I have followed you as far as I can,
darkness falls in the wood.

I touch your tree, I cannot reach you:
dry burrs and scales,
bark that scrapes my hands.

What will you do if I leave?
Grow dense and hard, sinking forever
inside the wood that holds you,
your face an effigy under the vines.

I feel myself stiffen like you,
an old mistrust driven like a thorn
into the tree of my flesh.

I will close this part of the forest,
bar the road with a thicket –
ivy or rhododendron,
something I know you loved.

No one will come, and no bird sing
from these shuttered boughs.

I leave with a living branch
seized from the wrack between us:
brand or torch,
green knot of desire
by which I will see my way.

(1974)

IN THE MUSEUM GARDEN

I
Always dying into ourselves,
coming back again into sunlight . . .
Your face beside me is a frieze
of shadows; many things
wake there and go to sleep.

I I
This day we walked through the galleries,
steeped in the glory of echoes.
A bitter dragon smoked on his pedestal,
the stone horses stolen from China
stamped in their marble fields;
under glass, one uplifted arm of Kali
seemed to me to tremble.

I I I
We halted before a mountain
towering in silk, climbed a pathway
footworn by the steep passion
of the anchorite; high on a bench
of hand-quarried stone we rested,
dreaming in a shower of blackbirds.

I V

There is so much flowering around us,
so much color burning the plum bough.
Summer, dense and smoldering
in the teahouse throng; your body,
part of a well-loved earth,
glowing in its printed sunlight.

V

And much that is dying. These faces
blurring to leaflight as we walk,
these words of water spoken
from the trees . . . City traffic,
that towering noise beyond the gate,
a speech already strange.

V I

We lean on the boredom of princes
who built their palace of air
and leaves, names signed in the stale
history of these halls and ledgers.

V I I

They left us wandering in a peopled
grove, listening at nightfall
to these grave echoes in stone:
our voices calm at this closing hour,
our own footsteps leaving the garden.

(1970–72)

THE LAKE IN THE SKY

Once more evening on the earth
lies awash at our feet,
the light of many wrecked suns.

Look down in this furnace of water
clearing of smoke:

our people are there,
black reeds erect or bending
upon the night,
each one afloat on his shadow;
now the fisherman
burns on his rock alone.

A figure flaming in oak leaves
stands here beside us;
he tells of ripening acorns,
and dust glittering at summer's end;
of someone lost on a mountain
plunging green in the west,
that far-off splashing.

Two beaver in the lighted depths,
sleek and afire,
bound for the shore of a cloud.
Swallows like flares,
soaring alive in the dark . . .
All that is left of the sun
is a red dog lapping the shallows.

Evening games, voices of men
and women parting in the dusk,
singing out of sunken campgrounds;
the firewheel turns, the light
from the ring on your finger darkens . . .

(1972)

PASSAGE

Between night and day a door
opens and closes in the wind;
a skin that separates, enormous
onion peeling in the twilight.

The dead go through without a sound,
the living squeak and finally pass.

A cricket sings on the other side;
he disappears, and a man
on one leg hops and falls,
his mouth shaped in a silent cry.

And everything depends on the stone
of passage, a small round stone
that you hold in your hand
to hurl at a barking stranger.

Death, sleep, and desire come from
a leaf smoked in solitude,
from a tall root ground to powder.

The daylong, breathless climb
to the endless plateau of twilight,
where sand lifts and the wind blows.

(1971)

DRIVING THROUGH OREGON

(Dec. 1973)

New Year's Eve, and all through
the State of Oregon
we found the gas pumps dry,
the stalls shuttered, the vague
windmills of the shopping malls
stopped on the hour.

The homebound traffic thinned,
turning off by the roadside;
I lost count of abandoned cars.

This is the country we knew
before the cities came,
lighted by sun, moon, and stars,
the glare of a straying comet,
sparks from a hunting fire
flying in the prairie wind.

The long land darkens, houselights
wink green and gold,
more distant than the planets
in fields bound with invisible wire.

We will drive this road to the end,
another Sunday, another year;
past the rainy borders of Canada,
the wind-shorn taiga,
to the shore of the Great White Bear;

and stop there, stalled in a drift
by the last well
drained for a spittle of oil.

The driver sleeps, the passenger listens:
Tick...tick...from a starlit engine,
snow beginning again,
deep in a continent vacant and dark.

(1974)

ROLLING BACK

For a long time now
we have heard these voices
singing along eroded wires,
murmurs from the veiled partitions
of clouds, little whispers
tracing the dust...

They tell us what we partly know,
hidden by the noise we make:
the land will not forgive us.

Crushed and broken things,
shapes of clay and burning lignite,
come from the soil of the plains
and speak to us their words in smoke—
the hawk of the nightmare
is flying again.

The past returns in the lightning
of horses' manes, iron shoes
striking sparks from the pavement;
in the idleness of men who circle
the night with their sliding ropes.

Everything we have known for so long,
a house at ease, a calm street
to walk on, and a sunset
in which the fire means us no harm...

Rolling back from the blocked summit
like an uncoupled train
with no hand on the brake,
gathering speed in the dark
on the mountain grade.

(1975)

ARLINGTON

The pallor of so many
small white stones,
the metal in their names,
somber and strange
the calm of my country.

My father buried here,
and his father,
so many obedient lives.

And I too in my time
might have come,
but there is no peace
in this ground for me.

These fields of death
ask for broken columns,
a legend in pitted bronze
telling of the city
pulled into rubble here.

The soil should be thick
with shrapnel
and splinters of bone;

for a shrine, a lamp
fueled with blood,
if blood would burn.

(1972)

CIRCLES AND SQUARES

So many painted boxes,
four walls, a roof, and a floor;
when you sit in their chairs
or lie in their beds,
the light of the sun goes out.

Ah, when everything was round:
The sky overhead, the sun
and the moon, galaxies whirling,
the wind in a turning cloud;
the wheel of the seasons rounding,
smoke and fire in a ring.

And the tipi sewn in a circle,
the cave a mouth blown hollow
in a skull of sand,
as the cliff swallow shapes
to its body a globe
of earth, saliva, and straw.

A square world can't be true,
not even a journey goes straight.
Bones are curved, and blood
travels a road that comes back
to that hill in my heart.

So many buried disasters
built squarely,
their cities were walls
underfoot or climbing.

My feeling for you
goes out and returns,
even the shot from a rifle
falls in an arc at last.

So many boxes; the windows
don't break soon enough,
and the doors never fail to shut.

(1972)

FOURTH OF JULY AT SANTA YNEZ

I
Under the makeshift arbor of leaves
a hot wind blowing smoke and laughter.
Music out of the renegade west,
too harsh and loud, many dark faces
moved among the sweating whites.

I I
Wandering apart from the others,
I found an old Indian seated alone
on a bench in the flickering shade.

He was holding a dented bucket;
three crayfish, lifting themselves
from the muddy water, stirred
and scraped against the greasy metal.

I I I
The old man stared from his wrinkled
darkness across the celebration,
unblinking, as one might see
in the hooded sleep of turtles.

A smile out of the ages of gold
and carbon flashed upon his face
and vanished, called away
by the sound and the glare around him,
by the lost voice of a child
piercing that thronged solitude.

I V
The afternoon gathered distance
and depth, divided in the shadows
that broke and moved upon us . . .

Slowly, too slowly, as if returned
from a long and difficult journey,
the old man lifted his bucket
and walked away into the sunlit crowd.

(1972–76)

VICTORIA

I

A girl, half Indian, seated
on a floor of beaten clay,
threading beads,
little knots of green fire
on a strand of sinew.

I I

I saw you standing in sleep
beside a horse, your face
turned down to the earth at your feet.

Then you were awake and astride
that horse, running eastward
through empty, half-lighted streets —
faster and faster,
a furious galloping past farms,
over stubble and waste allotments;
the dawn made shadows fly
on the early fields, a dream
filled with the sound of running.

I I I

Day of the sandhills stretched
before you, lit with leaping fires.
You wandered afoot there,
searching the scorched ravines,
marking the rivers, wallows
where the hot bulls rolled and steamed.

Once more the wilderness vanished,
taking flight in the leaf veins,
grass that when touched flew into ash,
burned sticks of animals,
the wind sounding in a storm of drums.

And as you stayed, fixed in the solace
of your dream, four gates closed

on the distances —
great trees of stone, splinters of light.

        I V
Dear friend at the continent's end:

Wilderness survives at the camp
we have made within us,
a forest filled up with night,
its ancient sounds
and floating, starlit images.

The sun climbs again, the landscape
wrinkles into shadowy ranges
and subsides; a plain of light
kindles in the morning haze,
dust from fallen pinnacles
and milling of beasts in the sod.

Will we ever again be at home
on earth? Great bale of straw
smoldering in the darkness,
mire stuffed with singing bones.

The green circle is broken,
life and dream scattered
through the flung constellations . . .

This rain of particles,
random sparks catching fire,
blowing out in the stellar drifts,
each one seeking the other.

                    (1 9 7 4)

TO MY FATHER

Last evening I entered a pool
on the Blackfoot River
and cast to a late rise,
maybe the last of a perishing fall.

Light shone on that water,
the rain-dimple of feeding trout,
and memory,
and the deep stillness of boyhood.

And I remembered, not the name
of the river, nor the hill
in Maryland looming beyond it,
nor the sky, a late rose
burning that eastern summer;

but the long, rock pool that whispered
before us, and your voice
steady and calm beside me:
"Try it here, one more time . . ."

And the fly with its hook floated down,
a small, dim star riding a ripple,
and the bright fish rose
from under its rock, and struck.

Last evening I watched a rise
break again on the still current;
quiet as a downed leaf,
its widening circle in the dusk.

(1974)

AT SLIM'S RIVER

Past Burwash and the White River delta,
we stopped to read a sign
creaking on its chains in the wind.

I left the car and climbed a grassy bluff,
to a grey cross leaning there
and a name that was peeling away:

"Alexander Clark Fisher.
Born October 1870. Died January 1941."

No weathering sticks from a homestead
remained in that hillside,
no log sill rotting under moss
nor cellar hole filling with rose vines.
Not even the stone ring
of a hunter's fire,
a thin wire flaking in the brush.

Only the red rock piled
to hold the cross, our blue car
standing on the road below,
and a small figure playing there.
The Yukon sunlight warming a land
held long under snow,
and the lake water splashing.

From the narrow bridge in the distance
a windy clatter of iron –
billow of dust on a blind crossing,
but a keen silence behind that wind.

It was June 4, 1973. I was forty-nine.

My ten-year-old daughter
called to me from the road:
she had found a rock to keep,

and I went down.

(1 9 7 3)

ROADWAYS

I

These images and their hidden voices
roused in me a sleeping child:

The great yellow van drawn to a curb,
our family chairs vacant on the lawn;
all those unreadable books
nailed shut, lamps now darkened
among the dead. Awakenings, true
and fabulous journeys; the shifting cars
of a train boarded at midnight,
then a vague ship shuddering west.

The dust of warehouses falls
through many drafty schoolrooms,
the hold of brief residence
let go in the shade of chimneys
lengthening on forgotten streets.

I I

Many times bound outward
from a house no longer mine
I waited with a freezing bundle,
rocked in the gusts from vans
hauling by in the snowy dark.

I learned an ancient track,
scar of the wilderness that sings
around lighted towns,

the rush of trees through starlight
on a stone planet rolling beyond
the dense prosperity of houses.

   III
Years ago my father read to me
pages lit by the beastlight
in a mountain cave: how we came,
shaggy and stuck with burrs,
but a hand and eye
striking fire in the limestone.

And how we went, a tribe uprooted
from ourselves, the road
all voices and transformations;
bewildering flux of shadows,
spokes, and a rim, the one
great mirror of water flashing.

   IV
It is morning again in the west,
clear and radiant under
these slowly scattering clouds.

Over a bridge of land
and restless water,
where the ox-cart axles
grind and wear,
the sun rolls its wheel of fire
through the squalor
of awakening eastern streets.

(1974)

Part VI

NEWS FROM THE

GLACIER

1982

THE SUN ON YOUR SHOULDER

We lie together in the grass,
sleep awhile and wake,
look up at the cloverheads
and arrowy blades,
the pale, furred undersides
of leaves and clouds.

Strange to be a seed, and the whole
ascent still before us,
as in childhood
when everything is near
or very far,
and the crawling insect
a lesson in silence.

And maybe not again
that look clear as water,
the sun on your shoulder
when we rise,
shaken free of the grass,
tall in the first green morning.

(1975)

HOMESTEAD

I
It is nearly thirty years
since I came over Richardson Hill
to pitch a bundle of boards
in the dark, light my fire
and stir with a spoon
old beans in a blackened pot.

II
What did I come for? To see
the shadows waver and leap,

listen to water,
birds in their sleep,
the tremor in old men's voices.

The land gave up its meaning slowly,
as the sun finds day by day
a deeper place in the mountain.

III
Green smoke and white ash,
the split wood smelling of honey.

And the skinned carcass of a fox
flung red in the snow, frost
flowering in the blue, flawed glass —
these are the images.

The canvas tent wall warmed
by a candle, my halfway house
of flies on summer evenings.

IV
One morning in my first winter
I met a tall man set apart
by the crazy cunning in his stare.

From him by tallow light
I heard his tales of Richardson
and Tenderfoot, names and antics
of the pathfinders and squawmen,
Jesus-workers, quick whores.

I followed where his hand
made a hill or a hollow,
saw their mark on the land,
the grass-grown scars,
fallen bailiwicks, and heaps
of iron scaling in the birches.

These shadows came and went.
One still September day
I knew their passing
left no more sound in the land
than a handful of berries
tumbled in a miner's pail.

V

From the spent dream behind me,
Dakotas, reeling Montanas . . .
came grass fires, and
a black hand mowing the plains.

The floor of the sky littered
with shackled farms,
dust through the window cracks,
a locust cloud eating the harvest.

California, pillar of sandstone,
Oregon still vaguely green –
these are the images.

And now on the high tundra,
willows and water without end,
come shade and a noise like death.

V I

Old ladders shorten, pulled down
in the sod, half-rotted houselogs
heaved by the frost; my hand
spans the distance I have come.

Out of a passion turned searing
and blind, like a theme
of bitter smoke, a deep blow
strikes at the granite roots.

By oil-light and the glint of coal,
forcing its way,

a rougher spirit invades the land,
this ruin carved by a plow.

        V I I
Here is the place I came to,
the lost bridge, my camp
made of shouldered boards
nailed to this hill, by a road
surveyed out of nowhere.

A door blows aside in the wind,
and a path worn deep to the spring
showers familiar leaves.

A battered dipper shines here
in the dusk; the trees stand close,
their branches are moving,
in flight with the rustling of wings.

                              (1 9 7 5)

BY THE OCEAN

We are here by the ocean,
the sun going down offshore
in the country of fog,
and night
building its ark around us.

We make our fire under the wave
of a log, prepare to sleep.
You, small and awake in the shadows,
read from a book:

the pages are air and smoke
printed with salt,
and the sea light falls
on your inland face.

The story of a people
moved by a voice in the wind,
crossing the land
to look once more at the sea.

The sea light and the firelight
reveal to them the passage
of men and stirring beasts,
starfish and star alike,
a rock like a ruined church.

The sea voice is old in our ears,
and fire is old in the
salt white roots of the tree.

I shift one charred, spent timber
and watch the last sparks
fly in the evening wind . . .

Ash from a driftwood fire
falls on your page.

(1 9 7 5)

WOMAN ON THE ROAD

It was in North Dakota,
and she walked the furrows
under poles half in sunlight
and the night-telling wires.

Winter was close to her hand
in the dry corn-stubble
of the fields, and the thin
elm shadows
falling behind her.

The distance held her, the brown
earth stretched before her.

She thought of the summer,
so distant now,
when she walked this way
crowded by the dense green
of the corn, and the wind
came to her full of the song
of the locust and lark.

So much was gone from her,
familiar as the coat she wore,
and yet she knew her way.
She climbed a little hill
and stopped there;
saw that the road went on,
that the air was keen
toward Saskatchewan.

And turned and walked back
to her house still in the sun,
as the calm fall made
a noise like a broken stick.

(1975)

THE EYE IN THE ROCK

A high rock face above Flathead Lake,
turned east where the light
breaks at morning over the mountain.

An eye was painted here by men
before we came, part of an Indian face,
part of an earth
scratched and stained by our hands.

It is only rock, blue or green,
cloudy with lichen,
changing in the waterlight.

Yet blood moves in this rock,
seeping from the fissures;
the eye turned inward, gazing back
into the shadowy grain,
as if the rock gave life.

And out of the fired mineral
come these burned survivors,
sticks of the wasting dream:

thin red elk and rusty deer,
a few humped bison,
ciphers and circles without name.

Not ice that fractures rock,
nor sunlight, nor the wind
gritty with sand has erased them.
They feed in their tall meadow,
cropping the lichen a thousand years.

Over the lake water comes this light
that has not changed,
the air we have always known . . .

They who believed that stone,
water and wind might be quickened
with a spirit like their own,
painted this eye that the rock might see.

(1975)

THE BLOOD LAKE

Hiking the Miller Creek trail
we came on a runnel of blood
in the snow, and saw beyond it
a small red lake in the road.

Blood of a deer shot last winter
when the hard frost rang,
hair and pine needles matted
together in the rotting ice:

a little lake
with its blood-soaked margins.

We looked long and deep,
quietly spoke of the killing,
and then went on.

At the far end of that valley
we found a great red barn
open to the weather,
belted and roofed with steel.

The cold red paint was fresh,
smell of turpentine and
ice in the wind.

(1974)

THE HEAD ON THE TABLE

The enormous head of a bison,
mineral-stained,
mottled with sand and rock flour,
lies cushioned on the museum table.

To be here in this bone room
under the soft thunder of traffic;
washed from the ice hills and blue muck,
skull and spine long since
changed to the fiber of stone.

One black, gleaming horn upswept
from the steep forehead,
eyelids sewn shut,

nostrils curled and withered.
The ear thinned down to a clay shell,

listening with the deep presence
of matter that does not die,
while the whole journey of beasts on earth
files without a sound
into the gloom of the catalogues.

The far tundra lying still,
transparent under glass and steel.
Evening of the explorer's lamp,
the wick turned down
in its clear fountain of oil.

In the shadow made there,
a rough blue tongue passes over teeth
stained by thirty thousand years
of swamp water and peat.

(1975)

THE GHOST HUNTER

Far back, in the time of ice
and empty bellies, I and three others
came over the tundra at evening,
driving before us the frightened deer.

We lighted small fires on the hillsides,
and heaped up boulders
at the gates of the valley.

We called to each other over tossing
antlers, beat legbones together,
and shook out bundles of hoofs...

There was a soft thunder in the moss
as the firelit meadow of bodies
broke past to the corral of the dead.

Now the long blade of the autumn wind
sweeps the willows and bearberries,
yellow and red in the evening light.

I hear nothing but the dinosaur tread
of winter, huge wingbeats in the stone.

I have come to this trampled ground,
to stand all night in the wind
with a hollow bone in my hand.

(1969–80)

ON THE MOUNTAIN

We climbed out of timber,
bending on the steep meadow
to look for berries,
then still in the reddening sunlight
went on up the windy shoulder.

A shadow followed us up the mountain
like a black moon rising.
Minute by minute the autumn lamps
on the slope burned out.

Around us the air and the rocks
whispered of night . . .

A great cloud blew from the north,
and the mountain vanished
in rain and stormlit darkness.

(1970)

NEWS FROM THE GLACIER

I

That mid-fall morning, driving north
toward Glacier Park,
we stopped above Flathead Lake
to see the fields and terraces
deep in a lake of mist.

An inland sea, risen by night
out of ponds and ditches,
silently lapped the hillsides.

And we who had slept for so long,
more than a thousand years,
awakened – to know the world
we came from by these vague fossils
held still in the fog:

grey masts of the heavy pines,
the half-roofs of barns
and houses, cattle standing asleep
in an air like water.

Nothing living or awake;
no wind, no sound,
and the light drained of color.

I I

Sunlight struck before us
at Marias Pass.

A pack train loading
by the roadside, horses
and red-shirted men
standing in the chill;

three mules already loaded,
roped and bound uphill,
splashing the icy shallows.

Like figures held over
from the day of stampedes
and vigilantes, another light
than this sun glinting
on the barrels and buckles.

Their tents still half
in the morning shadow,
smoke from that fire
winding up to the ridges,
thinning before the hunters...
And out of the sunlit,
steaming grass before us
a coyote bounded—

gone in the smoky thickets.

     I I I
We climbed all afternoon
up Avalanche Creek,
following a track in thin snow,
over roots, and loose stone
tunneled by water;

and came near evening
to a small, half-frozen lake
held in a cirque.

Snow was the dust on those peaks;
at the lake's far end
an orange tent
blazed in the mountain shadow.

I sent a stone skittering over
the ice, that made a sound
like a creature that cries in the dusk,
warning of night and the cold.

And we stood and listened
in the silence that echoed after,

to know what cried,
what bird, what thing that was.

        I V
Nine thousand feet in the Rockies,
staring into the blue vault,
we saw a cloud
form out of vapor and wind . . .

Swiftly a hurrying whiteness
spilled from the rock ledge
above us, and plunged,
terrace by terrace,
tearing itself into rain
and mist . . .

As if a whole summer held back
in the desolation of the sky
had spent itself,
foam and radiant bubble;

to lie regathered, quiet,
a blue pool staining
the yellow rock at our feet.

        V
West of Logan Pass, where
the snow held back another hour . . .

The mountain goats came down,
out of the cliffs above us,
down from their pasture
of sedges and lichen.

Small groups of them, bound
for water, shelter from storm;
snowdrops, small clouds
bringing their shadows to earth.

And seeing the people there
below them, they stopped
and quietly grazed out of sight
in a thorny thicket.

All but one old billy
who stood alone on the ridge,
his beard in the wind,
watching the watchers who
waited and stamped their feet.

We left them feeding
in the windy darkness
and went down, slowly
descending in loops of stone,
while the mountain turned
slowly white behind us.

V I

On a bend in the road near St. Mary
the rock wall gave back to us
the eroded shape of a whale,
something part fish or reptile
stranded here when the seas went down
and the mountains lifted.

Slowly the meat rotted, then water
came back, and sand piled again
on the windy skeleton.

Far above us in the remote divide
there are seams of sediment
packed with little shells,
stone surf breaking green and rose
in the high snow air.

The deep lake of the west is gone,
only this beached leviathan
sleeping here in the rock wall
slowly turns on the wide earth bed.

That spine has changed to quartz,
the bleached bones break
into fragments that cut our fingers.

V I I
Toward Many Glaciers,
where the granite coiled
in a gritty pattern,
like the thumbwhorl of a giant
imprinted when he strode
from the west, and paused:

Nothing much to see there
in the watery east, he braced
himself on this mountain,
skidding a mighty stone
over the flooded continent.

V I I I
East from Glacier Park
an immense herd lies buried.

Thighbones, blunt ends of ribs
break through the soil,
a little grass like hair
straying over them in the wind.

Whatever they were, Mastodon,
Great Horse, Bison
or something no one has named,
they were hunted down
by the cold, starved
in the great earth changes.

We read in this landscape
how they came and went:

Faces to the ground, feeding,
following the gusty ridges,
they had lakes for eyes,

and the future drained away
as they moved and fed.

IX
After the twenty thousand year
siege of rain and ice
the broken gates stand open;
a few rocks piled at the portals,
far plains strewn with bones.

From the long march overland,
scouring the rockwalls,
making camp at the foot of moraines,

we came to this sprawling
settlement of wind and dust,
these streets laid out
among the boulders, metal signs
pocked and flapping.

No great encampment stands in view
at Browning. We are awake
in our own desolate time –

clotheslines whipping the air
with sleeves and pockets,
little fists of plastic bags
beating the stony ground.

(1975)

HUNGER

I was born to this crowded waste,
came late in my time
to know the knot in my belly.

To read the soil,
a warning written in the rocks,

and formed in a book
of my own making
such wordless images
the earth gives up –

faces like broken bowls,
their mouths
stuck together with saliva.

Body and book of stone,
leaves cemented with slime
and weighted with clay.

Seeping through thousands
of pages, a stain
like green mud
thinned into water.

And I have seen myself
an animal, stripped
of all comfort,
not able to speak my name,

a terrified creature
gnawing at roots.

(1977)

THE FOSSIL

I

All spine and knotted fin-rays,
the great fishtail lashing
in a petrified stillness
where the seas are warm,
and life is beaked and nailed
and armed with teeth.

Caught in this green stone wave,
abundant flesh
uncoils from its spiral shell.

I I

Sometimes in our sleep
this grey, carnivorous shadow
comes drifting and feeding,
like the toothed smile
at the lips of living men.

A lighted spine lashing
uphill in the evening traffic,
home to the clay beds
where night after night
the heart's wide nets are cast.

I I I

Inside the shell of our skulls,
pink and buoyant tissue
held by the thinnest membrane,
tasting of salt . . .

Drawn to his thirsty depths,
the great shark feeds there still.

(1977)

MOTHBALL FLEET: BENICIA, CALIFORNIA

These massed grey shadows
of a distant war,
anchored among burnt hills.

The chained pitch and sweep of them
streaked with rust,
swinging in the sunlit silence,
hinges of a terrible labor.

Years before the last war
my father and I floated past them
on the Chesapeake:
our oarlocks and quiet voices
sounded in the hollow hulls.

And once again these shadows
crossed between me and the sunlight,
formations under flags of smoke.
They carried men, torpedoes,
sealed orders in weighted sacks,
to join tomorrow
some bleak engagement
I will not see.

They are the moving, the stationary
walls of my time.
They hold within them cries,
cold, echoing spaces.

(1977)

ALIVE IN THE WORLD

Stand still in the middle of the world,
let it be Missoula,
any crossroad in the west.

You are here, alive in this place,
touching with sight
things that are smoke tomorrow.

Go on into the surge of it,
this torrent of leaves swept up
from the maples swaying in pools
at your feet,
flung down once more to the gutters.

The sun comes briefly out of the storm,
lighting the alleyways,
their shingles and gleaming nailheads;

afternoon disappears into evening,
full of ghosts, torn spirits
in the wind, crying to be seen ...

Trees of the earth underfoot,
what all of us walk on,
shatter and pass through,
going blindly into our houses.

(1976)

MISSOULA IN A DUSTY LIGHT

Walking home through the tall
Montana twilight,
leaves were moving in the gutters
and a little dust ...

I saw beyond the roofs and chimneys
a cloud like a hill of smoke,
amber and a dirty grey. And a wind
began from the street corners
and rutted alleys,
out of year-end gardens, weed lots
and trash bins;
                        the yellow air
came full of specks and ash,
noiseless, crippled things that crashed
and flew again ...
grit and the smell of rain.

And then a steady sound,
as if an army or a council,

long-skirted, sweeping the stone,
were gathering near;
disinherited and vengeful people,
scuffing their bootheels,
rolling tin cans before them.

And quieter still behind them
the voices of birds
and whispering brooms:
                              "This land
has bitter roots, and seeds
that crack and spill in the wind . . . "

I halted under a blowing light
to listen, to see;
and it was the bleak Montana wind
sweeping the leaves and dust
along the street.

(1975)

HARVEST

There will be much to remember,
a load of wood
on your shoulders, a dusty
sack in your arms, full
of the smell of rutabagas
and winter cabbage.

For the paths are rough,
and the days come on
like driven horses.

But we have kept faith
with ourselves.

We will not look back
but press on, deeper
than the source of water,
to the straw-filled cave
of beginnings.

There in the vegetable darkness
to strike a match, kindling
the cold, untraveled sun.

(1962–80)

Part VII

NEW POEMS

1990

LITTLE COSMIC DUST POEM

Out of the debris of dying stars,
this rain of particles
that waters the waste with brightness . . .

The sea-wave of atoms hurrying home,
collapse of the giant,
unstable guest who cannot stay . . .

The sun's heart reddens and expands,
his mighty aspiration is lasting,
as the shell of his substance
one day will be white with frost.

In the radiant field of Orion
great hordes of stars are forming,
just as we see every night,
fiery and faithful to the end.

Out of the cold and fleeing dust
that is never and always,
the silence and waste to come . . .

This arm, this hand,
my voice, your face, this love.

(1983)

MEDITATION ON A SKULL
CARVED IN CRYSTAL

> After *is the wrong word. It is an entirely different*
> *dimension. Time and space are crystalizations out of*
> *God. At the last hour all will be revealed.*
> — MARTIN BUBER

I

To think that the world
lies wholly in this mind;
that this frozen water,
this clarity of quartz,
this ice, is all.

At home in the glass house
of wit, keeping watch
on the last conceit:

to say to oneself
in this fallen mirror
that the fog-drift of trees,
the inch of sky
in the well of windows—

these water-broken figures
entering and leaving
the last, drained pool
of light, are all.

I I

Within the artifact,
in the polished brilliance
of its mirror faces,
lies the bleached horror
of the empty skull
and its loosened hinges:

of the threadlike sutures parting,
and the drained blood
dried to this rusty scale.

Think of a house abandoned
to the cold chalks that score
the limits of dust:

the ear-ports catching wind,
the long porch of the nostrils
from which the watch-beetles
and the blue, predatory flies
have long since gnawed the solitude
and eaten the silence.

And where intelligence
kept its station,
arranging interior spaces,
opening windows toward
the shellshot lunar fields,
inhuman distances...

There is nothing to see
but a small, green hollow
holding rain.

III
Where there is nothing...

But the drained stillness
of thought, the quelled
and muttering life of stones —

that which in nature
brings on inertia,
passivity, and sleep.

Wind is not welcome,
fluttering the soul of things,

nor love that makes
the shadows couple and sway.

Nothing but death is here,

windless and calm – sheer
absolution in the slow
cementing of sand grains,

glass particles that spell out,
drop by drop, the fate
of water sealed in a jar.

    I V
No one the color of darkness
sees entirely the shape of the sun.

But as the ocelot goes, smoldering,
spotted with fire, through the night –

Go now, return to water and mist.
You of the fireborn, go back to rain,

be what in the beginning you were:
seed of ice and brother to grain.

You with the glass mouth, drink
more silence. Be watchful, an eye

upturned in the soil of heaven.
And every shower rebuilds your face;

at the heart of your stillness
the cry of a god trapped inside a star.

    V
Blood into ice, and fur
into matted frost –
this is the way of winter,
on earth as in heaven.

Divided nostrils that smelt
of blood from afar;
the throat that drank it,
the lips and the tongue
that thirsted:

changed into that which
is shone upon, that
which mirrors, and that
which sees if looked upon.

Nothing of beast or man
remains, of the stroked fur
and the aroused flesh;
but the filed teeth fixed
in their glitter,
a smile of ferocious peace.

   V I
Burn sacrifice, for all
that was clear has darkened
in the burning glass.

Break open the breast-cage,
let the creature-heart redden
in the light that remains.

Swear by the fallen blood
and burnt savor of the flesh
that the sun will rise,
that the wheel of the calendar,
carved with its lunar faces,
will never stop turning.

Put death aside,
there is nothing to fear
from the sleep-walk of spirits
in this darkness
not wholly of the night.

The great stone hall is quiet;
these pillars and dreaming cases
like a household
calmed at nightfall.

Now, as the smoke of sacrifice
disperses through chilled
and vacant rooms,
the white ash deadens and falls.

Sleep, for the changed heartbeat
knocks and is still . . .

In place of the lamp
that was lighted,
a drop of blood inside the sun.

V I I

As if the pain of thought,
by repeated blows, would be
nothing but light in the end.

Stare into this well of shadows,
drained and never empty:
all nomenclatures, measurements
by meter and inch forgotten.

Beyond the dark slates of water
and sunlight, how the stone
jaw slides on its hinges,
how the nostrils quicken,
and the glassy brow crowns
the eyes, sunken and gleaming.

All suns, all moons, all days,
find their completion here,
as blood finds its pool of quiet
where mercury sleeps, and night

with its pallor of threads
draws the sutures closer.

The cold hours pass;
a fire-seed fumes, blown
once more into life.
The star-crossed lattice
brightens; day begins,
as empty, as filled
with floating shadows,
voices waking as before.

    V I I I
Of the dissolution
of fabrics and structures,
the breaking
of cemented boundaries:

Improvisations – names
that vanish among
the catalogues that vanish,
all their complexities
strung with spittle:

Hierarchies, lists of the
flowering and cheeping world:
of these and what
we knew this life to be,

death is the last confusion.

After the smoky anguish
of your dying
comes this resolution:

the opening calm, a blue
thoughtbound space
in which there are signal
lights, globed fires
giving way to night.

IX
Intelligence is what we find,
gazing into rock as into water
at the same depth shining.

Mirror, glazed forehead of snow.
Holes for its eyes, to see
what the dead see dying:

a grain of ice in the stellar
blackness, lighted
by a sun, distant within.

(1977–86)

TENDERFOOT

It is dusk back there, the road
is empty and the log house quiet.

Jessie, the Indian girl, stands
at the doorway in silence,
her thin face turned to the earth.

No more than an aching shadow,
her father bends at the sawhorse,
cutting the last dry pole.

The swallow box has fallen,
the catalogue has lost its pages.

The black mouths of the rain barrels
are telling of migrations,
the whispering rush
of a lonely people toward the past.

(1962–82)

RAIN COUNTRY

> *Earth. Nothing more.*
> *Earth. Nothing less.*
> *And let that be enough for you.*
> — PEDRO SALINAS

I

The woods are sodden,
and the last leaves
tarnish and fall.

Thirty-one years ago
this rainy autumn
we walked home from the lake,
Campbell and Peg and I,
over the shrouded dome,
the Delta wind in our faces,
home through the drenched
and yellowing woodland.

Bone-chilled but with singing
hearts we struck our fire
from the stripped bark
and dry, shaved aspen;
and while the stove-iron
murmured and cracked
and our wet wool steamed,
we crossed again
the fire-kill of timber
in the saddle of Deadwood —

down the windfall slope,
by alder thicket, and now
by voice alone, to drink
from the lake at evening.

A mile and seven days
beyond the grayling pool
at Deep Creek, the promised

hunt told of a steepness
in the coming dusk.

I I

Light in the aspen wood
on Campbell's hill,
a fog trail clearing below,
as evenly the fall distance
stretched the summer sun.

Our faces strayed together
in the cold north window —
night, and the late cup
steaming before us . . .
Campbell, his passion
tamed by the tumbling years,
an old voice retelling.

As if a wind had stopped us
listening on the trail,
we turned to a sound
the earth made that morning —
a heavy rumble in the grey
hills toward Fairbanks;
our mountain shivered
underfoot, and all
the birds were still.

I I I

Shadows blur in the rain,
they are whispering straw
and talking leaves.

I see what does not exist,
hear voices that cannot speak
through the packed
earth that fills them.

Loma, in the third year
of the war, firing at night

from his pillow
for someone to waken.

Campbell, drawing a noose,
in the dust at his feet:
"Creation was seven days,
no more, no less . . . "
Noah and the flooded earth
were clouded in his mind.

And Knute, who turned
from his radio one August
afternoon, impassioned
and astonished:
         "Is that
the government? I ask you —
is *that* the government?"

Bitter Melvin, who nailed
his warning above the doorway:

Pleese dont shoot
the beevers
They are my friends.

    I V
And all the stammering folly
aimed toward us
from the rigged pavilions —
malign dictations, insane
pride of the fox-eyed men
who align the earth
to a tax-bitten dream
of metal and smoke —

all drank of the silence
to which we turned:
one more yoke at the spring,
another birch rick balanced,
chilled odor and touch

of the killed meat quartered
and racked in the shade.

It was thirty-one years ago
this rainy autumn.

Of the fire we built to warm us,
and the singing heart
driven to darkness
on the time-bitten earth –

only a forest rumor
whispers through broken straw
and trodden leaves
how late in a far summer
three friends came home,
walking the soaked ground
of an ancient love.

V

Much rain has fallen. Fog
drifts in the spruce boughs,
heavy with alder smoke,
denser than I remember.

Campbell is gone, in old age
struck down one early winter;
and Peg in her slim youth
long since become a stranger.
The high, round hill of Buckeye
stands whitened and cold.

I am not old, not yet, though
like a wind-turned birch
spared by the axe,
I claim this clearing
in the one country I know.

Remembering, fitting names
to a rain-soaked map:
Gold Run, Minton, Tenderfoot,
McCoy. Here Melvin killed
his grizzly, there Wilkins
built his forge. All
that we knew, and everything
but for me forgotten.

    V I
I write this down
in the brown ink of leaves,
of the changed pastoral
deepening to mist on my page.

I see in the shadow-pool
beneath my hand a mile
and thirty years beyond
this rain-driven autumn.

All that we loved: a fire
long dampened, the quenched
whispering down of faded
straw and yellowing leaves.

The names, and the voices
within them, speak now
for the slow rust of things
that are muttered in sleep.

There is ice on the water
I look through, the steep
rain turning to snow.

(1978–83)

DEATH AND THE MISER

Remember that time *is money.*
— BENJAMIN FRANKLIN

I

God surely sees us,
for He sends His messengers
when we lie dying,
tugging in a repentant fever
the gold seams of a shroud.

Remember, if you can,
in your drenched delirium,
the pinched rancor of the hours
spent sorting and weighing:
the squint, the measuring grasp
fastened on dust, flake and coin.

And now the last lock is sprung,
and the domed lid
of your counting-chest stands open.

And see: the swollen purses,
rubbed and darkened leather
spilling great seals and rings;
the lure of swindled clasps
loose in their amber or ruby light.

And tossed among these,
like so many bitten leaves
tied with black thread,
the sordid bundles of credits,
foreclosures, and mean accounts
cannot be hidden.

Be sure the deadly creatures
that litter the floor
with their glittering excrement
will find you. With six and eight

polished, segmented arms
they climb the sills, horned
against the casement light.

There will never be time
to try all the keys,
nor will you be strong again
to wrestle the weight
of these belted doors that close.

So pull the shroud to your chin,
let go of your wallet
and stop your ears,
as with his steely, measuring
click
        click
                the gold-eating
beetle of death
                climbs nearer.

        I I
The dream within the acorn,
still green at the heart
of the forest, had more substance
than that closet-sleep of yours,
shut in by more than
natural earth and lumber.

Your rents and your reckonings,
meticulous in subtraction;
your ledger locked at nightfall,
as if all life's guilty
confusion were cancelled
by that sleeve-worn shelving
and quiet turn of a key.

From soil of soot and paper,
the sand you sifted over
the blotting ink of your days,

came neither fruit nor flower,
nothing feathered but a pen,
nor wind-shaken whisper
above the arid rustling
of your thumbed, exacting pages.

There, by candle or fretted sun,
you might have seen, as now,
flickering and doubled by fever,
your shadow-self at work,
cowled and booted,
and with great butcher's shears
slitting the rose of mercy
into a thousand tatters.

I I I

You would never willingly wear
the clothing of the dead,
nor touch their flesh, soured
and damp and printed with leaves.

And yet each day you have filed
and sorted the claims of death,
cut paper death in the morning,
signed ink death in the evening.

The list of death:

Ledger-death and curtain-death.
The death that studies,
that sits in chairs and stands
at counters:
                    Death the receiver.

Death in a rented cassock: cleric
and lender, the ape of stations.
And early each morning he offers
to the cold knees of penury
his wafer-death and credit-death.

For death is a shadow-priest
leaning at his slotted window;
no more than a voice, sabbath −
darkened, whispering of penance
and absolution:

> Death the confessor.

And death is waiting overhead;
he coughs, spits in the sand-wake
of voices receding. The last
of the spilled earth falls, and soon
the gardener's tread, crisp
and single on the unraked leaves.

I V

Believe in the angel beside you,
his patient and willing gesture:

> (Death with a letter
> to be delivered)

Believe in the cross, whose wood
is tinder, whose nails are rust:

> (Death with a fiery pencil
> will pierce you)

Believe in the light blown forward
from the darkness behind you:

> (Death with a windy lantern
> will find you)

Believe in the rote of numbers
chirped from the cloister at evening:

> (Death with the reed of the
> vesper sparrow is calling)

Remember: God surely sees us . . .
He rocks and smokes in His office:

    (Death in a quiet slipper
    will open the door)

    V
So much leaden weight,
so much desire turned inward.

To follow without hope
of turning, the animal-reek
of one's own track . . .

And no one to call you back
from its steep momentum –
into the black rain
of ink, the fury of hurled
buttons and fiery quills.

And of the self-mounted
lashed to a standstill,
you too will know their anguish,
their late remorse,
who from the rank spring
of their hearts drink thirst,
only to drink again.

As yoked and branded cattle,
stunned with the blood
of the killing-floor,
they know the yelp and cutting
rein of the deputies
who ride there – masters
of pain, tyrants of the split
hoof and cloven brow.

    VI
Be comforted, for your companions
go with you

down the difficult stairs.

Not creatures of your mind alone,
neither men nor women
nor angels – but stooped
and pilfering
they swarm about you
with cold beaks and probing
snouts – quarreling
rodents, insects
as large as yourself.

And their voices that are no voices,
but like the sounds of things
broken underfoot – crushed leaves
and littered shells –
thicken the air you breathe
with muddy whispers,
suppressed whines
and stifled barking.

And God is nowhere now,
if ever He watched
and crossed you
with His wand of ashes.

But waiting in their grounded flight
stand towering birds
whose outspread wings
appear to be fanning a fire,
and yet it is cold,
the frost of a thousand
winters of iron.

And deeper still as you go,
on every side
now rise before you
and fall away,
the round and rolling
shapes of gigantic coins,

tall keys with eyes
giving off sparks in the gloom . . .

These, and the ringing,
metallic shadows of Death,
who is himself a miser —
once he has taken,
he never gives anything back.

(1980–84)

DAYS OF EDWARD HOPPER

Of such may be the simplifications that I have attempted.
— EDWARD HOPPER

I
These are the houses that stand,
broken and entered; these
are the walls written by rain,
the sparrow arches, the linear
stain of all that will one day
turn to smoke in the mind.

Brick dust was their pigment,
mortar and the grit of brownstone
ground underfoot, plaster
flaked to the purity of snow.

And out of these we entered
the glass arrangements of wind,
became the history of sunlit,
transient rooms, domestic shades;
a substance volatile, so thin
the light of stations burning
at the roadside consumed us . . .

And out of that, the stillness.

II

Dusk, and the fiery gospels
tried in the faith of Tums,
tobacco leaf and cereal boxes,
once again are lighted . . .

Totems in lumber, standing
ovations for the sun-bleached
faithful signed aboard
the everlasting vacation.

The night shuttle lurches
on its dizzying track,
a beast of iron and cinders.

Three . . . four . . . echoing flights
into the rusty azure,
hourly the platform trembles,
the coach windows flash . . .

Dawn in the stairwell climbs
and falters. It is evening,
dimmed to a paper lampshade
tilted beside a chair
where a man is reading,
methodically turning his pages.

He finds there, both comic
and deadly, all that he needs
of his coin-deciphered world;
the key to its club-mythologies
and funhouse games,
a dream logic steeped in profits . . .

Endorsements, white sales
that wink and vanish
under the signs in rotation
stopped cold in ashes.

III

Tell me, you who were close
to my heart, how of so
much sleep and forgetting
came that brief and
quarreling peace we knew?

From the drone and the rote
of a meticulous boredom,
only a stifled outcry
heard by the night custodian.

History was a name to give
confusion its contours —
so great a darkness of mind
scrawled with the writ
of governors, agents, and clerks,
to which we spoke aloud —
one hand on a baffled heart —
to name but not to question.

So much for this child
of amazed colonials,
deceived as to the shore
they claimed; so much
for the citizen who
with such passion swore
allegiance to tar sands.

I think the long, barbed
shadow of a street lamp
troubled the night walker
home to his household.

I think the barber pole,
a flag without stars,
with no consoling blue,
striped the patriot
shorn in his revolving chair.

IV
Obedience to Sundays drilled us
to march in the flag days
that followed; but nonetheless
were fragrant and rosy with knees,
and one could savor at recess
the evening tilt of small breasts
cupped under knitted sweaters.

The blue lines checked with red
crossed upon a page relentless
in the direction of protractors,
triangle squares: *the law of,*
the root of, the stem of . . .

Obedience to numbers moved us
to cherish whatever could be added
or taken away: uncertain hope
in the solace of lunch pails
and the fortune of sand lots.

All that in time was sanctified,
pure beyond all censure,
upheld our life, our sweetness
and our hope. From that strict
sodality of white wings
and black cowls, this benediction
under the rule of a handbell
rung in the red brick frost.

V
Sleepwalker, your footsteps
long since were ground to echoes
in the glassy pavement.

Smoke was the emblem for manhood,
then as now; and *Gasoline*
the name of our country –
high octane that fueled

a tribal frenzy in the music
we danced to, the manic
vacancies we took for joy.

Our cinematic consolations
from which the Neverlands
were built – radio voices,
blackface prophecies,
tight hands and sweating lips.

But there were no words to speak
for the refused passion of a girl
standing at the porch rail
under the moth-ringed light.

We kept from the lessons learned
of many querulous masters
no more than was written
on the leaves we raked
to the curbing and burned
in the swift October night.

V I

A trolley bell clangs
in the distance,
the control lights change,
and around the circle
with its chained
and blackened monument
the traffic wheels
and charges –
carriages and horses,
primitive cars.

And evening, corrosive
with inner light,
comes the stone-slotted
benches where the elderly
are seated –
dry catarrhal crickets,

rustling their papers,
minding their dogs.

The darkness reaches
toward them out of the trees
and flowering shrubs:
they do not see it,
not one of them understands
how soon, how swiftly,
the grass at their feet,
the paths by which they came,
the words on their lips
will vanish.

V I I

I think of those desolate,
captive years, the labor
of their confident speeches,
their stale decorum
and conscript gestures
of the upright dead.

Of our imperfect, stammering loves,
their guilt and their silence.
Our grasslit campaigns,
in which we studied
the insect life of helmets,
fables of our natural fathers.

Whatever it was we talked about,
roaming the urban dark;
whatever in that lawful night
preserved us – cheap wine
and stolen smokes, our pulse
in the hand-tooled engine
idling at the curbside.

All that in time preserved us,

before the hammer of war
and the rake of wealth
that followed, when the arm
of the paid sleepwrecker
pulled the nails and swept
it all – brick dust,
peeled paint and plaster,
into the great steel dumpster.

VIII

And once for me also,
when quarreling whispers
were abroad, the damp wind
of an autumn night
blew the one sheer curtain
aside.
           Light that signaled
the end of a game begun
by the earth's wise children
came with its slow red pulse
to the room where I lay
awake, dismantling night.

Long knives of the shadows
slit the walls. A news-throat
muttered interrogations
at the rain-frontier: names
of the still-to-be-missing,
the sold, the bloodied
and trampled – small peace
and unforgiven crime.

(1981 – 91)

HEAD OF SORROW, HEAD OF THOUGHT

You would think that no one
had the right to so much
distance and calm.

And yet how often do we see,
clouded and still,
the face of someone gone
out of himself
into stone or water?

The rider in the train,
escaped into the glass fields;
the watcher in the garden,
changed once to a leaf,
now to the cold light on a pond.

Face of the storm, we say,
we have faced you,
heard you howling within,
quelling the atoms
of a bruised, exacting heart . . .

She, who out of the tempest,
came to this calm,
gazing as if from a distance
made equally of granite and cloud.

(1 9 8 5)

OF MICHELANGELO, HIS QUESTION

Sybil and prophet have spoken,
are fixed in their chairs:
Your strength was in your thought,
your dream your answer,
your consummate gift your pain.

Muscular night stands over Persia;
once more the whirlwind sweeps
the dark-tongued leaves
to the lap of a woman so old
she is a child who cannot remember
when her book of the marvelous
came unthreaded
and the pages were scattered.

Long ago the rainstorm of heaven
abated; the sun-dried witnesses
marked between the ark-ribs
God's majestic finger
stirring the dust of Adam.

A trumpet blew, one mighty event
was promised: the dead awakened,
to be ranked and divided –
the damned and the anointed,
equally made of earth.

But to stand four hundred years
in a courtyard, a pillar
for birdlime: your shoulders
warped, the stone in your hand
withheld for the one
antagonist yet to come . . .

Then, and only then, one's dream
would die into clay and rubble.
To prayer and petition
God speaks the simplest words:
sun, rain, and *frost.*

Here, at the end of the corridor,
where night and dawn,
dusk and noon, are gathered
in the one standing tree,
art and history
compose their towering image.

To this cloudlit stillness
the pilgrims come, reading
prayers from a guidebook –
to see, to question, and depart.

(1984–87)

ON A CERTAIN FIELD IN AUVERS

> *There is something in my heart . . .*
> – Van Gogh

      I
On the road to Hallucination,
pass by the yellow house
that is the house of friendship,
but is also the color of madness . . .

Stand by the roadside, braced
in the punishing wind that blows
on that field and another . . .
In the red dust of evening,
ask yourself these questions:

'Who made the sun, strenuous
and burning?'
        It was I.

'And the cypress, a green torrent
in the nightwind?'
        It was I.

'And the clock of evening, coiled
like a spring? . . . Who turned
the stars in their sockets
and set them to spinning?'
        It was I.

On the road to the Night Cafe,
where the light from a door
that is always open
spills over cobbles and tables;

where the pipesmoker calmed
his fury, a yellow chair
in which no one is sitting . . .

It is no one. It is I.

I I
I, who never for one hour
forgot how the light seizes
both field and striding sower;
who held my hand steady
in the solar flame, and drank
for my thirst the fiery
mineral spirit of the earth.

Who remembered always, even
in the blistering south,
a cellar in the north
where a handful of stunted
people peeled their substance
day by day, and all their
dumb and patient misery
steeped in a cold green light.

On the road to the hospital
built of the great stones
of sorrow, and furnished
with chains and pillows . . .
In the red dust of evening
the Angelus is ringing.

And out among the haystacks,
strange at this late hour,
a light, both moving and still,
as if someone there was

turning, a ring of candles
burning in his hatbrim . . .

It is . . . no one.

   I I I
In the Asylum of Saint-Rémy,
that is also the burnt field
of Auvers; at the graveside
of two distracted brothers.

On this one day in July
we speak the rites for all
torn and departed souls.

And we hope that with
a hundred years of practice
we have learned to speak
the appropriate words:

'In the country of the deaf
a one-eared man was king . . .

'In the name of the poor,
and of the holy insane,
and the great light of the sun.'

                    (1 9 8 6)

PAOLO AND FRANCESCA

Only they who have found in love
and longing for the flesh
their entire being,
will understand this prolonged
anguish of flight
through a lasting midnight.

There was death, brother of desire,
who came with a sword.
And hate, crowned with a mighty
will. Passion's book
that was opened, and the story
once begun, lived out to the end.

And who, having met, kissed
through forbidden pages
the slime-stained mirror of love.
Who broke the glass
and followed the fire within –
hurled together
into the muttering starlight...

And such arousal as lovers know
who find in that staring
wakefulness, refusal of sleep,
vigil and consummation.

(1985)

BROKEN MIRRORS

> ...of what is not visible.
> – PICASSO

I

If what you saw of the majestic
crowing cock of the world
was loud and clear, a metallic
brightness beaked and strutting...

When in that glittering moment
illusion was still intact,
and sunlight on the glass
of the river was broken
by nothing but raindrops...

And there was coupling
in the dark of the garden
by gaslight, and all that
swirling, impetuous throng
was bright pretence,
glamor and savage paint . . .

What then was reality
in a world invaded by mirrors,
whose glass would break,
whose splinters pierced
the dry heart from within?

I I
Into your blue forgetfulness,
distant with clowns,
silent in the wake of tumblers,
came these crippled hordes —

a thousand fractured faces
with stunned eyes that strayed
from corner to corner,
to be fixed in a brutal stare
that had no smile behind it . . .

As if all of humanity's clipped
cartoons and holy discards —
composure of sleek madonnas,
breasts and buttocks, the leaping
limbs of centaur and faun —
were hacked and crumpled,
shaken in a box, and a voice
in all that litter cried out:

I I I
"I . . . I . . . am the woman,
the face on the playing card,
I the lightbulb, and I
the skull of a stricken horse . . .

"I sit in a room with no one
to talk to, I play the clown,
ride the circus bicycle
round and around in a circle . . .

"I dance where the splinters
are green, I break into smaller
and smaller needles of red . . .
But I stop, stop in my giddy

"gyrations – Stop, listen
to the blind guitarist
who goes on playing, though
his music cannot be heard."

I V

But when all these shattered
faces are halfway mended,
and the horrible, stabbing beak
of the world is blunted,

you return once more
to an enormous blue room,
where the clowns are distant
and the wheels are still.

Dazed and famous
in your small white age,
you will sit by the hour,
to stare with filmed eyes

on the one bright image composed.

(1986)

THE OWL IN THE MASK
OF THE DREAMER

Nothing bestial or human remains
in all the brass and tin
that we strike and break and weld.

Nothing of the hand-warmed stone
made flesh, of the poured heat
filling breast, belly, and thigh.

The craft of an old affection
that called by name the lion shape
of night, gave rain its body

and the wind its mouth – the owl
in the mask of the dreamer,
one of the animal stones asleep . . .

By tinker and by cutting torch
reduced to a fist of slag,
to a knot of rust on a face of chrome.

So, black dust of the grinding wheels,
bright and sinewy curl of metal
fallen beneath the lathe:

Speak for these people of drawn wire
striding toward each other
over a swept square of bronze.

For them the silence is loud
and the sunlight is strong.

No matter how far they walk
they will never be closer.

(1984)

ANCESTOR OF THE HUNTING HEART

There is a distance in the heart,
and I know it well—
leaf-somberness of winter branches,
dry stubble scarred with frost,
late of the sunburnt field.

Neither field nor furrow,
nor woodlot patched with fences,
but something wilder: a distance
never cropped or plowed,
only by fire and the blade of the wind.

The distance is closer than
the broomswept hearth—
that time of year when leaves
cling to the bootsole,
are tracked indoors,
lie yellow on the kitchen floor.

Snow is a part of the distance,
cold ponds, and ice
that rings the cattle-trough.

Trees that are black at morning
are in the evening grey.
The distance lies between them,
a seed-strewn whiteness
through which the hunter comes.

Before him in the ashen snow-litter
of the village street
an old man makes his way,
bowed with sack and stick.

A child is pulling a sled.

The rest are camped indoors,
their damped fires smoking
in the early dusk.

(1 9 8 3)

WATER OF NIGHT

> . . . *The naked trees,*
> *The icy brooks, as on we passed, appeared*
> *To question us, "Whence came ye, to what end?"*
> — WORDSWORTH

I

Before any match was struck
or a candle lighted,
someone spoke well of the sun.

There were bones to read
while the long dusk lasted,
marrow to force with a stick.

Feather of auk, beak of owl,
were tools to work the shadows,
make the winter hawk fly
and the stone ox stand.

As sparks fly seaward
from a beaten driftlog,
telling the days of a journey . . .

So from its mitten a hand
cracked with frost
parted the mosswick flame,
to read in a shoulderblade
the source of smoke
and meaning of the wind.

Nothing was written for the snow
to keep or the water
to carry, nothing to be forgotten.

And one man late in his years,
by light of the sun
through a wall of ice,
carved from ivory
a weasel the length of his finger.

II

The night people called to the shadows,
and the shadows awoke —
came down from the rafter clearings

in the light that came at sundown,
slowly basking,
from the fires at earth's end.

The night people spoke in whispers,
or with the cries of storm-driven birds
— wings in the darkness overhead
bearing homeward the souls of the dead.

And the dead were awake, upright
and listening,
in the tread of the striding wind.

*

Then came the steady lamp,
and the reader
solitary in his pages.

The night people fell silent,
their lips were crushed,
shadows flew home from the walls . . .

Light, abundant light
has killed them, great books
have put them to sleep.

III
From a few rocks ground into powder,

refined sugars dissolved
burning on our tongues,
from a yellow corrosive flour
we made our bread.

Our crumbs and our crusts,
thrown out, blew away . . .

to the feet of the sparrows
who pecked them,
to the knees of the homeless
who clutched them.

It was part of what we did not know
and put aside,
a bread better eaten in silence
with greying faces.

From these once more
came death,
by water, by wind.

Invisible dust from within
began to eat up our bodies.

IV
When the people of shadow
were burned,
their ashes changed into flies
and stinging swarms.

Full of blood as winter came,
they returned to the earth
and slept.

And so the deep changes went on:
fingers into roots,
and rocks from their clinging bones.

But the people of shadow
would not lie still;
they shouldered their atoms under snow

for the sweating farmer come back
with the sun
to break his furrows.

Each turn of his plow,
a swarm of ashes
rained upward from the ground.

V

After the burden of soil
was set aside,
and the scouring shovels halted,

in the great trenches
a little rain fell,
soaking the coal dust.

A wind came over that land
and its white hills moved,
the thin grass seeded there
could not hold on.

Slowly, like a surf on the plains,
tumbling and foaming,
pushing the farms,
the battered, unpeopled towns:

houseframe and headboard,
grey barns shattered to lumber,
with snarls of stockwire
bound into tossing bales . . .

Came on with blowing sand
and stones rolling,
with nothing to stop them,

into the souring trenches,
the black ravines.

VI

We who found work for the dead
knew how to build,
from the clay of the land
and the lime of their bones.

Effigies in mud stood by
and watched us, cemented in labor:
little teeth, glinting nails,
and the bones remembered.

They ate into the silence
of the priests, studied oppression
in the bowls of the beggars;
gnawed and listened
until the halls blew empty.

Famine, wind of the prophecies,
a dryness invading the fields;
great, smothering trees
climbed the eroded chancels.

Strange men who read the past
stopped here with pencils,
deciphering shells, to be told
by a grimace from the leaves
how all this dust went by:

We, the stone herdsmen,
driving before us in a fever
the cattle of rock
and the sheep of sand.

V I I
Fire that was sunlight
blackened in the fields of earth,
dry lake and smoldering reef,
deep fernwood drowned in night.

A saw-tooth locked in that grain,
the shell body of a beetle
still rasps in tundra pools.

Seeds, brown flesh of leaves:
an old fragrance of the forest,
a sour reek and ash
blown down from chimneys.

V I I I
Each of us brings a shadow,
another self we carry
as long as we walk in the sunlight,
and a dead thing's shadow dies.

Dry heads of thistles
make a shadow,
the stretched figure of a man
standing or striding,
wire, and a blade of straw.

Shadows into pools, and pools
into lakes flood back,
windlass ropes hauling darkness
out of foaming wells:

comes up with sound of frogs
and the night cries of birds,

strong blood of something
killed in the earth.

And these shadows are climbing,
big hands on our walls,
sticking and sucking...

Over the drowned gullies,
houses, fields of the earth,
seething and rocking,
water of night.

(1 9 7 7 – 8 2)

IN THE FOREST WITHOUT LEAVES

> ...*Believe me, he alone*
> *is interesting who still*
> *loves something.*
> – JACOB BURCKHARDT

I
In the forest without leaves:

forest of wires and twisted steel...

The seasons are of rust
and renewal,
or there are no seasons at all,

only shadows that lengthen
and grow small –
sunlight on the edge of a blade.

Nothing that thrives, but metal
feeding on itself –

cables for roots,
thickets of knotted iron,

and hard knots of rivets
swelling in the rain.

Not the shadows of leaves,
but shadows where the leaves might be.

        I I
What sounds can be heard
in a forest without leaves?

The freezer-mutter that talks us
to sleep:

The teeth in the rubber-chatter
that nip us and wake us:

From zone to zone, veering
and halting, a frantic bleating
from the sheep-wagons:

The road-hounds, red-eyed
and yelping:

And over the tree-tops,
snorting fire,
gas-bark and chopper-bite:

Wired and winking in sleep,
even the deaf repeat
the bright, green chirp
of the dial-crickets:

Da-deet, da-deet,

        Da-deet, da-deet . . .

III

This earth written over with words,
with names, and the names
come out of the ground,
the words like spoken seeds.

What field, what dust,
what namesake for a stone
that moves by inches
and clears a path in the mud?

Ice moved once, a river of stones,
and the road it drove
through the forest can still be walked.
Look there – you will find
for your house a standing boulder.

Earth worn deep by its names,
written over with words:

there are spaces inside those words,
and silence for the clearing
where no house stands.

I V

One rock on another,
that makes a wall.

One field by another,
one house and another:
smoke, and the
dungfires at evening.

Voices, tread of a loom
in a doorway,
one thread and another.

A stick in the ground
and a hole for the seed,

and one stone
rolled on another.

One child and another,
one death by another:
earth, and the
funeral pyre at evening.

The men of mud
came to plow,
the people of dust
will harvest.

          V
Earth speech:

the furrow sighing
behind the plow,
the clods talk together.

Mobs of dust protest
in whispers,
pushed on by the wind,
and the spilled sand
hisses, going by.

Talus, those rough words
spoken by mountains
growing old;
young pebble voices
make noise underfoot.

The cry of a rock
loosened in the night
from the cliffs above,

rolling past.

V I
And sometimes through the air
a cone of dust,
once flower, tree, or child . . .

Takes sudden fire across a field,
a running shape
that falls to nothing in the wind.

You cannot say what name it had.

And sometimes through the air
this dust is like a willow
tethered to a cloud . . .

It burns before us, glittering
in the sun,
to vanish on the road.

And sometimes through the air
a thing of dust . . .

V I I
Say after me:

I believe in the decimal,
it has divided me.

From my tent of hair
and the gut-strings that held it;
from my floor of grass
and my roof of burning cloud.

I have looked back across
the waste of numerals –
each tortured geometry
of township and lot –

to the round and roadless vista,
to the wind-furrow

in the forest track
when I had myself entire.

Say after me:

That freedom was weight and pain,
I am well-parted from it.

Earth was too large
and the sky too great.

I believe in my half-life,
in the cramped joy
of partitions,
and the space they enclose.

VIII

Building with matches,
pulling at strings,
what games we had.

Monopolies, cartels,
careers in the wind,
so many tradesmen of dust.

Steam in the kettles,
blades in the cotton —
big wheels went round.

And soon there was nothing
but lots and corners,
the world chopped to pieces.

Each piece had a name
and a number,
thrown in a box:

games given to children,
they too might learn

to play –
grow old and crooked,

fitting the pieces,
pulling at strings.

    I X
Those who write sorrow on the earth,
who are they?

Whose erased beginnings still
control us – sentence
by sentence and phrase by phrase,

their cryptic notations vanish,
are written again
by the same elected hand.

Who are they?

Remote under glass, sealed
in their towers
and conference rooms –

Who are they?

Agents and clerks, masters
of sprawl –
playful men who traffic in pain.

Buried in their paragraphs,
hidden in their signatures –

Who are they?

    X
Life was not a clock,
why did we always measure
and cramp our days?

Why the chain and why
the lock,
and why the chainman's tread,

marking acres and stony squares
out of the green
that was given?

To see in a forest
so much lumber to mill,
so many ricks to burn;

water into kilowatts,
soil into dust,
and flesh into butcher cuts—

as we ourselves are
numbered, so many factors
filed in a slot.

Say after me:

The key that winds the clock
turns a lock
in the prison of days.

X I
How the sun came to the forest:

How the rain spoke
and the green branch flowered:

How the moss burned
and the wasp took flight,
how the sun in a halo of smoke
put an end to summer.

How the wind blew
and the leaves fell.

Death made a space in the forest
where snow would come,

and silence, and night.

XII
In all the forest, chilled
by its spent wealth,

in the killed kingdom of grass
where birch leaves
tumble and blow;

(and over the leaves is written:
how great the harvest,
how deep the plow)

I know one truth:

Nothing stains like blood,
nothing whitens like snow.

XIII
What will be said of you,
tree of life,
when the final axe-blow
sends your great wood crashing?

Something about the wind upstairs,
that tromping and thrashing
on a roof never still?

What of the rift in your rafters
parting, your nests
and shingles flying?

What trace of your winter shadow,
but a lean, fantastic spider
sprawled and knotted in the snow?

And no one left to tell
of your heartwood
peeled down to a seed of ash,
your crowned solitude
crushed to a smoldering knot...

The ages parted to let you fall,
and a tall star blazed.

X I V

A coolness will come to their children,
the solar wind falling calm,
a stillness in the sun.

The poles swing wide into darkness,
there is ice in that distance.

In the deep stone shell of the suburbs
candles are stirring,
a tallowy stain on the drifts.

Humanity thinned to an ancient hardness
strikes scant fire
from the wood of buried houses,
speaks of soil and spring
with frost-thickened tongue.

It is equinox, the time of old calendars,
when birds set out on their polar journeys,
whales turned north,
men thought of the plow and the net.

Snow is falling, the sun is late,
and someone has gone with a lantern
to search the roads.

X V

In the forest without leaves
stands a birch tree,
slender and white.

For the sun drank pallor
from its leaves,
and the marrow in its roots
froze down.

Only the paper bark stayed
to weather and peel,
be sunlight or tinder
burned in the hunter's fire,

and wind took away all the rest.

If and whenever we come again,
I will know that tree.

A birch leaf held fast
in limestone ten million years
still quietly burns,
though claimed by the darkness.

Let earth be this windfall
swept to a handful of seeds —
one tree, one leaf,
gives us plenty of light.

(1977–84)

Part VIII

NEW AND

UNCOLLECTED

POEMS

1993

THE POEM WITHOUT MEANING

"The spittle of the silent stars..."
           – GONGORA

We have been building it for
thousands of years, this emptiness
where grief is blowing,

a gust from a frozen fountain.
History is now undone, on a field
where red giants and white

dwarfs oppose each other, clash
and bestride the dust.
An immense horse grazes there,

trailing a thread of spittle.
He draws no chariot,
he runs no race, riderless

in the great cloud of himself.
Through a forest of electric trees
comes now an alien force –

a wind off the farthest glacier,
the haunt of huge auguries,
arms whirling, catching at space.

Remember now, St. Luke and the Ox:
how the mute and docile creature
kneeled to be instructed...

And as the saint was reading, intent
on his fabulous words, the page
before him burned to a black hole.

There are no more ballads, wiry
and pitched to the stars;
no aerial stages, no strutting boards.

No stretched and glittering figures
with the names of heroes,
heroes with the names of men . . .

All speeches of pith and grandeur
put away with weights and measures
in the deep mind of God.

Words spoken in the winter of Mars,
in the dusk of Saturn,
compose themselves . . .

The poem becoming Night.

(1964–92)

IN THE SLEEP OF REASON

And so I closed that book,
laid down the pen
and closed my eyes.

What had I thought to find,
reading by the light of cyphers,
abstract and piercing
in their constellations?

Nothing that night and the wind
could not have told me,
had I raised my head,
dimmed my lamp, and listened –

I, a thoughtful man, prone
to the dust of bindings,
coughing in the dry sequence
of verse and chapter
(for I had reasons).

And while I was sleeping,
came a small beak at my heart,
like a thorn, insistently
probing . . .

And I in terror awoke,
to know in that room
a tread ceaseless and pacing.

As if from within my being
came this upwelling,
of brute and shouldering forms:

heavy and beastlike, buoyant
and birdlike, but nothing
I could name, they moved
at ease, about and within me . . .

creatures of the starlight,
but also of the mind,
harbor to wolf and warlock.

So much do I remember now:
the pulse of obedient hearts,
hot tongues licking
the night; and I heard,

like a dry wind over leaves,
the scaly rustling of reptiles
coiling and resting . . .
All turned in the lamplight

eyes that never turned from mine
in their bright interrogation
(for I could see them,
and yet they were not there).

And I would speak, my hand
upheld to shield me,

when the shutter clapped
and my lamp blew out –

(was it a natural wind,
or a spirit-breath
lifting the leaves
of heavy trees in the night?)

And all subsided in the hush
that followed, in the calm
of great wings folding
and shadowy forms lying down.

I rose and left that room,
the house of my grief
and my bondage, my book
never again to be opened.

To see as once I saw,
steadied by the darkness
in which I walked
and would make my way.

(1986–90)

PROPHECY

How to live, when the only life
is one long triumph of engineering?
When today or a week tomorrow

doubt in the great perfections
tugs and whispers; and after auguries,
among the factions at nightfall,
one more knife is counted –

when there is only foreign earth
to conquer, and soon or late
the empire must meet a wall.

You will repeat from a history
beginning: *I came, I saw . . .*
the thrift of murder refined,
true justice in terror returned.

You will be for unruly colonists
a terrible kindness imposed,
adept at the bending of treaties,

wise in the numbering of innocents.
First among looters, go back
to Rome, to see by torchlight
the highroad strung with crosses.

And in spite of great wealth,
a good name, the obedience
of a wife married for reasons,

you will always be waiting
for what you do not know,
knowing that when at last
it appears you will not know it;

as under a strange, wandering
star, foretold, three men
of the desert will come to tell you.

No god awake in the household,
but a name and a rumor; nothing
of the spirit, but sometimes
a cold wind at the threshold.

No face but that of a slave,
with the soul of a slave,
and the grinding rut of pride.

(1 9 8 6)

A GUIDE TO THE ASIAN MUSEUMS

Footbound beneath the owl kings,
princes of darkness and striding priests
who go before us, leading
the dead in their hempen shrouds,

we learned what our crowned,
uneasy fathers learned:

That to be strong you must crush
the darkness underfoot,
break the back of your enemy
and snarl,
raising a fist to the light:

That a stone axe under glass
holds its edge, its weight and purpose:

That a small green scarab,
placed in the grave,
was a better guide in life after death
than the code of the gospels.

As it was in the Prophet's thronged
and holy city, sun-pillar
and moon-arch will be provided,
straw for the ox
and a tree for the serpent.

And a place at night for the lovers,
tumbled and ruddy with dust,
but who smile and hold each other,
who keep intact
their lesson in abiding passion.

From all our heaped arrangements
to comfort the dead
we have learned this much:

That the least of these fired images,
these flawed souvenirs – items
of rescue, of luck,
obedience and grace – outlast us.

That a single grey elephant,
the size of your thumb,
holds up the earth
with its forests and acres of stones.

(1 9 8 6 – 9 2)

THE SLEEPWALKERS

And the time that was given
to Egypt was Sleep,
and they who walked there
were called The Sleepwalkers.

Strode on through burning dust
in the blue-fired glaze of summer,
through unfailing flood,
through sandstorm and sunstroke.

To be, to sleep, to awaken . . .
that was the gift of an insect.
With the glittering eye of a hawk
and the beak of an ibis,
with the rasping tongue of a dog;

but stronger than any of these,
the law of drift and silence
overheard through reed-whispers
and unstilled barking.

Twilight, the one returning kingdom,
vaster than daybreak,
the unroofed temple where scribe
and monkey-priest sorted the strings

of birds; on a thread of smoke
the clay spirit climbed,
born of the light and the lotus.

And then, in the green heart
of stone, to sleep at last.
Among the restless, the sun-driven,
to be the one cured and stationed
man: Lord of the death-watch.

And night was a cobra, coiled
in the doubled knot of eternity;
symmetrical in sleep,
but steeped in poison, waiting
for the first king to wake

(1985)

THE FATES

Atropos o el Destino
– GOYA

North is east, south is west,
first is under and over
the last – all of our spells
our spilled and lost.

We are the swallows you see,
whose tongues are cut,
whose wings are clipped,
bunched on a wire.

And we are the spinster angels
driven from God:
we have saved our scissors
and kept our needles –

four old women who knit
and knit the winds,
and then in a muttering rage
unthread the clouds.

We are done with porches
to sit on, finished
with trees and branches.

Daylight for us was bad,
but night will be better:
star and planet falling,
lion and scorpion down ...

Think of your rooms
and your furniture,
make up your beds
and pocket your keys:

You that have shadows
will keep them, you
without shadows will die:

Here is the glass we look
through, and these
are the holes we make:

And now the threads we warp
and twist, the words
we spit, the spell we throw ...

(1985)

TONDO OF HELL

Everything we can think of to name
is encircled here, bound
with the darkened and rolling sun
to the wheel of a wayward wagon.

A bonfire raging in the distance
reminds us that our days
are brief and given to thirst,
and death by hanging consoles us
for the little luck we had.

High on a slope beneath the gallows,
Christ and his fugitive apostles
are sprawled and casting lots . . .

And as their idle custom proves,
so an ill wind blows
from the rotting thief.

And everything within and without
is turning – these flamelit episodes
in which we are audience,
actors, and substance . . .

          Slowly revolving,
the wheel of death in life
turning the mirrors of Wrath,
of Lust, Envy, and Pride,
to what remains of light on earth.

Hell has no exit –
not through the smoke ring
nor the fire door,
and not in the black wake
of the Arch-Priest
dissolving himself in ink.

And though we smirk and laugh
and pinch each other
in the grand, commiserable joke,

out of the din of agony
comes another, more sodden

sound: the buttocks
of the slothful beaten hard
with a four-foot spoon.

(1 9 8 5 – 9 2)

THE NIGHT THAT RYDER KNEW

Night is coming to the islands
of Maine, pine-shouldered
in their smoldering slack;
the sea with the smoke of a mountain
breaks the mirror of Katahdin.

To the gull with closed eyes,
drowned among bottles and combs,
this greyness of wing
and breast and cheek,
washed in the cold salt shallows.

Night is coming to the chalked houses
with their plain drawn blinds.
And to the people
grown quiet in their rooms
without lamps or shadows,
seated and staring,
hands on their heavy knees.

The night that Ryder knew,
great molten wave
with all its sea-lights burning.

A cold and sweating horse
gallops inland from the wreck
of Time, overturning
as he runs, salt of pillars
and paint of stalls . . .

To the pale, muted track
where Death is riding,
and all the trees are white.

(1984)

HOMAGE TO DAVID SMITH

We are made of angle iron and crossbrace,
we live and we die
in the sunlight of polished steel,
in the night of painted iron.

All that surrounds us and by which
we will be judged –
these incompleted circles,
perforated diaphragms,
gnawed shields, unfinished arrows –
will be taken as signs

pointing inward to an iron self,
or else toward the scrapyard
to which we seem to be rolling –

great studded wheels grinding
over the pavement,
leaving behind us crushed glass,
pieces of flattened tin.

And riding the space-drawn carriage,
as if they were weighted
and bent in a terrible heat,

five fixed and glowing figures
who are not men.

(1980)

THE BURGHERS OF CALAIS

Now if ever it is winter in the heart,
all hope withdrawn, and the mighty
siege unbroken. Stray faggots to burn,
whispers of straw, and rats to eat . . .

But where in God's stony kingdom,
in what broken province, stands
the market for so much knotted pain?

What commission for this torn
and heavy parting, this drained
confusion, this half-turned
forwardness in its wintry terrain?

Someone has paid for the rope
that binds these shoulders; frayed
and shortened, it was sold
by the yard, allotted in anguish.

And somewhere the fire that seared
the cradle to pour the metal
of shirts for these massive limbs,
these bared and planted feet,
cramped hands gripping the icy keys.

Flesh that is iron, stone
that is flesh. This one clutching
his face, who will not look up,
as if from the mire at his feet
he would raise his beaten homeland.

And he who turns to look once more
homeward, half-eager to catch
one farewell signal of smoke;
and he who measures the distance
still to walk, implacable, resigned . . .

Landholders!
                    Bellringers!
Merchants
                    and Lenders!

You that in duress delivered
to the mailed and haughty English
these six self-chosen men —

bound together in divided hope,
drawn forward over the cold
bronze field, to death or pardon.

(1984–91)

DIMINISHING CREDO

Eugene Delacroix, in your black hours
did you watch the painted vistas
closing, the hour of the hero strike
and wane? While down the boulevards
the night armies strolled
with banners, pikes, and slogans . . .

On the selling of souls followed
unnatural gifts. And did Mephisto,
your evening friend, track you
over the cindery rooftops, believing
that in your charmed, tormented
heart he had struck a bargain?

For it was you, Eugene Delacroix,
set fire to the great divan,
who locked the doors, cried smoke
to the household; and silent
screams swelled the tumult where
Sardanapalus burned, crazed
and driven as all kings are in the end.

And it was you lay prone, face down
on the loosening raft of empire,
adrift with those strange souls,
your countrymen, betrayed to hope,
unequal thirst in the salt blood.

And maybe for a last time you climbed
the scaffold, to trace as on
an airy field, some waking terror
born of the countryman's dream:
gave *Force* an obedient lion,
and *Justice* a woman's regarding face.

Attila, the cyclone, sweeping Italy,
Apollo in his sun-chariot
nailing Python in her smoky depth;
and Jacob, under satanic trees
wrestling for his passage . . .

I know of no replacement for the horseman
astride his destiny, nothing equal
to his flashing saber and his dubious
valor — no horse of metal, no lion
mute and chained to its pedestal.

Under your hand for one last time
the animal torso quickened,
aroused from sleep to fury;
and with you also an old dream
of the barricades flickered
and the map of history vanished.

It was the time of the photographer
and his flat, grey field,
the time of ascending balloons . . .

(1 9 8 4 – 9 0)

AGE OF BRONZE

I

Say goodbye to the arm
of the prophet, to the hand
or the fist upheld,
to strike and then to fall;
to the hammer dropped
and the anvil sunken.

To know that what we loved
for so long, the slope
and the shining – desire
in the green flesh
that found in every mortal
gesture a passion multiplied.

I I

Then if ever it was morning,
when the saints glittered
in their fiery glass, and out
of holocaust a burnt rose
dropped its petals in the wind.

God was a well in the rock,
an anchor in the cloud.
His stunned avatars,
sleeve-worn, heavy of purse,
watered the altar wine
and snuffed the candles;

the Magi and the oxen, driven
to forage in the feedlots,
and not long after,
the chapel windows blinked
through the arc of shellfire,
and the belltower fell.

III
A great spider of tin has landed.
Deliberate, humming an arid tune,
he grips the field, then
strings his netting in the sun.

Prophet of no faith but that
of dew and metal in the grass,
he glitters as he knots
his lesson, cryptic and true:

When the age of bronze is over,
the day of smoke begins.

(1985–92)

TO THE WALL

To the wall that holds up night
come these chained, myopic figures:
the faded nominees, envoys
without portfolios, past presidents
and shunted candidates...

Heroes with guttering torches,
ill-starred drummers
in the thickets of policy.

They stand, hollow and waking,
trying to see through
the coarse fabric of illusion;
and fall, as another volley
echoes in the reddening
canyons of our dawn planet.

And the wall advances,
trailing its broken ivy,
hour by hour,

with the sound of wind
through a slot.

May all the laboring captains,
junkmen, raiders and dumpers
— life-wreckers
whose seared lips blow
on the forges of sunset,

stand before that wall.

(1973–90)

STALLED COLOSSUS

El Gigante
— GOYA

I
So you stand to your waist
in a painted cloud at evening;
stand there and face another,
no more a lump or a stick
than you are, but a man
of the earth like yourself.

And with clubs, with rods
of iron, or with fists knotted,
deliberately swinging,
you rain these heavy blows,
mortal and telling,
upon each other's shoulders.

II
Beneath you, the evening,
the fire-colored earth,
a field disputed, fought over,
but still your own;
as from seeps and ravines

crawl, creep, or run
such fugitives as hell would know.
The cloudy, uncertain light
does not permit us
to say if they camp or vanish.

I I I
And there comes to that deafened
height at which you reel
(you and that violent other),
from somewhere within,
or from remoter distance,
the sound of gunfire –

a dull, prolonged concussion,
as through the wadding
of enormous books,
histories thick as mattresses.

I V
Now a sudden, bright applause:

and the air of sunset
swells to a floating pageant,
a balloon facade – a theme
of slowly revolving tapestries
printed with slogans:

Dead Branch

Ridiculous Folly

Courage – Against Corpses

And It Can't Be Helped . . .

Enigmas, seductions, for an audience
of clowns and princes

who from their cloud-balconies
look on, vacant, bemused,
as through the spaces among them
file the cloaked,
anonymous figures of death.

V

And a thing that is stranger,
more terrible still:
as if to say that earth
does not contain its fugitives,
but that they multiply
and break into virulent forms . . .

So now the twilight sings:
a wind-struck moaning
from the goat-mouths of people
transfixed in a circle —
a bundled and buffeted mass
who sway as if they would flee;

and yet they stay, instructed
by a creature that brays
as it tries to read
from a book held upside down;
the pages stick and tear
like leaves from a tree
stripped in the flooding darkness.

VI

And you, driven to your knees,
a thing shattered, earth-bitten —
you that are you, myself,
and so many others — cry out:
call, shout, whimper . . .
But there is no one now to face you.

You are the stronger, the rougher,
the uncontrolled, and under

the fierce rain of your blows
that other (your brother)
has fallen;
he lies without head, trunk,
or shadow, part now
of the one resisting element,
the mire and the pain.

    V I I
The cloud passes.

You rise, alone with your welts
and bruises – your blood,
your steep and violent night;
you stand alone, facing
the stone forehead of heaven,
like a mountain
no one can hope to climb.

                    (1 9 8 6 – 9 1)

NIGHT

Do not wake me, for I am not ready
to speak, to break the spell
fixed in these sleeping stones.

Go quietly here. Whisper to wise men
what you cannot speak aloud.
Quiet the metal of doors.

It is the time of earth-changes,
of vanishing rainfall,
and the restless barking of dogs.

Divided is the man of hidden
purpose, and evil his redemption.

Harness the wind and drive the water,
you that govern,
who yoke and stride the world . . .

And then be still.

Leaves of the one standing tree
fall through the twilight;
the nightborn images rise, the owl

in the mask of the dreamer wakes:
Who is the guest?
Who is it who knocks and whispers?

As one calmed in his death-dream
would never return
to this hunted world –

one more key to the clockwork
that drives the stunned machine,
another cry under the wheel . . .

But calmed and stationed aloft,
delight in his distance,
to see on the star-pavilions

the bright, imperial creatures rise,
ascend their thrones, rule
and prosper. The thrones darken,

earth in the moon-shadow fails,
and he alone in that cold
and drifting waste keeps alight

memorial constellations . . .

So I in this quiet sleep of stone
can say to you: Leave to me
this one sustaining solace –

my night that has more night
to come. To the sun that has set,
whose dawn I cannot see . . .

Mute in my transformation,
and do not wake me.

(1 9 8 5 – 9 2)

NOTES

PART II:

Guevara (page 52) Ernesto Guevara, Cuban revolutionary figure, who was killed in Bolivia in 1967.

A Dream Of The Police (page 53) Two historical events lie behind this poem: the storming of the Winter Palace in St. Petersburg in 1905; and the Massacre at Wounded Knee, South Dakota in 1890. The two events came together for me as the result of a dream I had in the late 1960s when the Vietnam War protests were so prominently in the news.

The Middle Ages (page 60) The chief reference here is to the well-known etching by Albrecht Durer, "The Knight, Death, And The Devil."

It Must All Be Done Over . . . (page 62) The title of this poem is taken from a brief essay by William Carlos Williams in his book, *In The American Grain*. The final stanza of the poem refers to a poem by the Polish Poet Leopold Staff recalling the chimney smoke of the Death Camps.

Cranes (page 63) The primary image in this brief poem refers to the immense flocks of sandhill cranes that gather annually over the Tanana River during their fall migration.

PART IV:

Mushroom Fable (page 88) The poem is in part a catalogue and a play on names. The words in italics are all common or regional terms for certain well-known types of toxic wild mushrooms.

PART V:

The Incurable Home (page 100) I wrote this poem shortly after the death of my father in January, 1969. The last line of the poem was adopted as the title of a musical work by the composer John Luther Adams.

Leaves And Ashes (page 109) The central image in this poem concerns the burial of her husband's ashes by a woman I knew only briefly. Coming as it did at the time of my own father's death, and at the end of the turbulent 1960s, the event struck me as having special significance.

The Whistle Column (page 110) The poem resulted from a particularly vivid dream. It and the poem that follows, "Peter's Start", concerned most directly my six-year-old step-son, Peter.

The Whale In The Blue Washing Machine (page 114) The poem was inspired by a dream told to me by my oldest step-daughter, Blair.

Jonna (page 118) This poem resulted from a single spellbound moment preceding an evening class at the University of Alaska, Anchorage in the spring of 1973, while listening with a young woman student to a recording of a poet reading his work. The poet was Robinson Jeffers.

Daphne (page 118) This and the following four poems concerned a woman I knew whose name, personality, and behavior at the time reminded me strongly of the Greek story of Daphne and Apollo. The conjunction was unusual in its intensity, but proved to be fortunate for the poems that came of it.

Passage (page 125) This poem was written shortly after reading the first book of Don Juan by Carlos Castaneda, part of a series popular in the late 1960s and early 1970s. I have forgotten now which details in the story prompted me to write.

Driving Through Oregon (page 126) The date, December 1973, marks the time of the first serious gas shortage in this country. At the time I was driving north to Seattle from California.

At Slim's River (page 135) A large glacial river draining into Kluane Lake in Yukon Territory, Canada. Burwash and White River are place-names in the same area.

PART VI:

Woman On The Road (page 145) The poem was inspired by a newspaper photograph I saw at the time, and which showed a woman walking alone on a country road in North Dakota.

The Eye In The Rock (page 146) The immediate occasion for this poem was an arrangement of prehistoric rock paintings at Painted Rock Point on the west shore of Flathead Lake in western Montana.

The Head On The Table (page 148) This poem originated with a color photograph of the head of a prehistoric bison shown lying on a table in the basement of the Smithsonian Museum in Washington, DC.

News From The Glacier (page 151) This nine-part sequence resulted from two trips by auto into Glacier National Park in the fall and early winter of 1974

The Fossil (page 157) I composed this poem after seeing the intact, well-preserved skeleton of an Ichthyosaur mounted on the wall of the Natural History Museum in York, England.

Harvest (page 161) This poem echoes, and is in part a translation of, a poem entitled "Erntezeit" ("The Harvest") by the German romantic poet, Friedrich Hölderlin

PART VII:

Meditation On A Skull Carved In Crystal (page 166) This long
   poem resulted from a visit to a branch of the British Museum
   in London in the spring of 1977. One of the primary objects on
   display is a larger than life-size human skull carved in pure
   rock crystal, and said to be of Aztec or Maya origin. After my
   first visit to the museum I wrote a brief poem about the skull.
   Much subsequent thought, and further reading in Meso-
   American mythology and religion, over a period of several
   years, brought the poem to its present length.

Rain Country (page 173) This poem, and the shorter one preced-
   ing it, "Tenderfoot", form a kind of elegy to a time and place,
   the Richardson-Tenderfoot area on the Tanana River south-
   east of Fairbanks, where I lived for well over twenty years. The
   poem names specific places in the surrounding country, as well
   as a few of the individuals known to me who lived and died
   there.

Death and the Miser (page 178) A small painting by Hieronymus
   Bosch in the National Gallery in Washington, D.C. Details in
   the painting compose an entire symbolic history of the life and
   fate of one individual, presumably a moneylender. Anyone fa-
   miliar with the Catholic faith will recognize references to cer-
   tain church practices, especially the confessional.

Days Of Edward Hopper (page 184) This poem in eight parts owes
   its existence to a few representative images in the work of the
   American painter Edward Hopper. The characteristic subjects
   of Hopper's paintings—the hotel rooms, the gas stations, cafes,
   and theater interiors—were all familiar scenes in my boyhood
   during the 1920s and the 1930s. The poem, then, is essentially
   autobiographical, and should not be read as an interpretation
   of Hopper's work as such.

Head of Sorrow, Head of Thought (page 191) The titles given by
   Auguste Rodin to two of his portraits of women.

Paolo And Francesca (page 195) The famous story of the two
   doomed lovers whom Dante meets in *Canto V* of the *Inferno*.

The Owl in the Mask of the Dreamer (page 199) This poem is a con-
   centrated history of the art of sculpture, from early times to
   the present. The last three stanzas refer to a famous metal
   sculpture by Alberto Giacometti.

In The Forest Without Leaves (page 207) This poem of fifteen sec-
   tions was originally projected to be part of a much longer se-
   quence that would have included the eight sections of the pre-
   ceding poem, "Water Of Night." For a number of reasons I

was obliged to alter my original conception. Perhaps the single most important factor in that decision was my collaboration with the composer John Luther Adams on a choral work for which the sequence now called "Forest Without Leaves" served as a libretto. At that point it was clear to me that this sequence of poems should stand alone. I later arranged the remaining poems under the title, "Water Of Night."

PART VIII:

The Poem Without Meaning (page 221) The poem in its present form developed over a period of 26 years from an early version published in the *Hudson Review* in 1966. Major references in the poem include: the Great Horse Nebula, the winter figure of Orion, and a stone sculpture of St. Luke from a church in southern France. The saint is shown seated with a book in his hands, while an ox kneels before him as if awaiting instruction.

In the Sleep of Reason (page 222) Reference is to a well known etching by Goya, "The Sleep of Reason Brings Forth Monsters." The poem is conceived of as being spoken by a scholar of the 18th century.

Prophecy (page 224) The poem refers to a typical Roman governor, of a mentality typical of empire builders and magistrates, now as then; in this case, one unaware of the dissolution of the old order and the coming of a new age as symbolized in the birth of Christ.

The Sleepwalkers (page 227) The poem is a summation of certain aspects of Egyptian mythology and religion. The poem contains also an oblique reference to the German writer Harmann Broch and his major novel, *The Sleepwalkers.*

The Fates (page 228) This poem is in part an interpretation of one of Goya's etchings in the series called "Los Disparates." The poem is imagined as a kind of riddle, or spell.

Tondo of Hell (page 229) Reference is to a painting by Hieronymus Bosch, one of the *Seven Deady Sins.*

The Night That Ryder Knew (page 231) The primary reference here is to the work of the American painter, Marsden Hartley, and particularly to his paintings of the Maine seacoast.

Homage to David Smith (page 232) The American sculptor, and a particular work of his in the Hirshorn Museum in Washington, D.C.

The Burghers of Calais (page 233) The famous sculpture group by Auguste Rodin. As rendered here, symbolic of a universal condition, common to exiles and refugees throughout history.

Diminishing Credo (page 234) Reference is to the work of this artist, his time and historical condition; perhaps the last great master of fresco painting.

Age of Bronze (page 236) A well known early work by Auguste Rodin. The poem is a condensed history of Western art.

Stalled Colossus (page 238) In the immediate background of this poem are two of Goya's so-called "Black" paintings. In part IV of the poem some of the titles given to individual etchings in Goya's series, "The Disasters Of War," are quoted.

Night (page 241) The poem is spoken in the voice of a sibyl, or oracle, as represented here by Michelangelo's immense reclining female figure of *Night* in the Medici Chapel in Florence. Into the base of the sculpture are carved both a tragic mask and the figure of an owl. Asked once what his figure of *Night* might say if she could speak, Michelangelo replied that she would say, "Wake me not . . ." Reference in the poem is also made to an incident in the life of C.G. Jung who, when once on the point of death, had a dream in which he found himself stationed far in interstellar space from which he could look down on the earth and its human events, completely detached. A return to life and consciousness plunged him into a deep depression.

TITLE AND FIRST LINE INDEX

ABOUT THE AUTHOR

Born in Norfolk, Virginia in 1924, John Haines studied at the
National Art School, the American University, and the Hans
Hoffman School of Fine Art. He homesteaded in Alaska for over
twenty years. He is the author of several major collections of poetry;
a collection of reviews, essays, interviews, and autobiography,
Living Off the Country (University of Michigan Press, 1981); and
a memoir, *The Stars, the Snow, the Fire* (Graywolf Press, 1989).
He has recieved numerous awards, including two Guggenheim
Fellowships, a National Endowment for the Arts Fellowship, the
Alaska Governor's Award for Excellence in the Arts, and most
recently a Western State Arts Federation Lifetime Achievement
Award and a Lenore Marshall/*The Nation* poetry prize for *New
Poems 1980–88* (Story Line Press, 1990). He is currently a free-
lance writer and teacher and still spends part of each year in Alaska.

This book was designed by Tree Swenson.
It is set in Imprint type by the Typeworks and
manufactured by Edwards Brothers
on acid-free paper.